Damon Young is an A̶u̶s̶t̶r̶a̶l̶i̶a̶n̶ ̶p̶h̶i̶l̶o̶s̶o̶p̶h̶e̶r̶ ̶a̶n̶d̶
commentator. He is an Honorary Fellow in Philosophy at the
University of Melbourne and the author of several books including
Voltaire's Vine and Other Philosophies. He lives in Melbourne with his
wife, son and daughter. Visit his website at: www.damonyoung.com.au

The School of Life is dedicated to exploring life's big questions:
*How do we find fulfilling work? Can we ever understand our past?
Why are relationships so hard to master? If we could change the world,
should we?* Based in London, with offices around the globe, The
School of Life offers classes, therapies, books and other tools to help
you create a more satisfying life. We don't have all the answers but
we will direct you towards a variety of ideas from the humanities
– from philosophy to literature, psychology to the visual arts –
guaranteed to stimulate, provoke, nourish and console.

How to Think About Exercise
Damon Young

MACMILLAN

First published 2014 by Macmillan
an imprint of Pan Macmillan, a division of
Macmillan Publishers Limited

Pan Macmillan
20 New Wharf Road, London N1 9RR
Basingstoke and Oxford
Associated companies throughout the world
www.panmacmillan.com

ISBN 978-0-230-76776-8

9 8 7 6 5 4 3 2 1

A CIP catalogue record for this book is
available from the British Library.

Cover design by Marcia Mihotich
Typeset by seagulls.net
Printed and bound by CPI Group (UK) Ltd,
Croydon, CR0 4YY

Visit **www.panmacmillan.com** to
read more about all our books and to
buy them. You will also find features,
author interviews and news of any
author events, and you can sign up for
e-newsletters so that you're always first
to hear about our new releases.

For my exercise partners: Ruth, Mike and Greg.

Contents

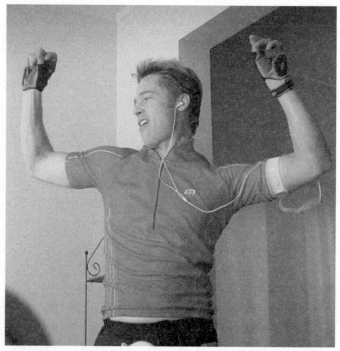

Chad: personal trainer.

Introduction

Meet Chad. Chad is a personal trainer, from the Coen brothers' film *Burn After Reading*. He is a fictional character, but we recognize him immediately: muscular, handsome, full of energy and positive thinking – and as dumb as a sack of small stones.

In fact, Chad is worse than a bag of pebbles, because pebbles are supposed to be dense. Chad has *made* himself this way. How? By living the life of the body. Chad is a professional jock, and his mind is forfeit. ('The hard body as soft brain,' as one *New York Times* reviewer put it.)

In this, Chad is a symbol of much that is missing in exercise today. His caricature, the idiot athlete, is such a common part of popular culture we can forget its meaning. It is not about this footballer or that tennis player, not a bias about buffed celebrities. It is not really about Chad and other personal trainers. It is a basic prejudice about human nature. The Chad stereotype comes from a conflict: between the mind and the body, thinking and doing, spirit and flesh.

This prejudice is behind the myth that sports stars must be stupid, and philosophers or writers weak and anaemic. It is an outlook that sees physical and mental exertion as somehow in conflict. Not because there is too little time or energy, but because existence itself is seemingly split in two. There are 'body' people and 'mind' people; 'flesh' places and 'spirit' places – and to choose one is to forgo the other. This is what philosophers call 'dualism', and it can rob exercise of its lasting appeal.

Mind: the Gap

To get a clearer idea of dualism, it helps to step back about four hundred years before Lycra shirts and 'get pumped' workout play-lists. Chad is probably not an avid reader of seventeenth-century French philosophy. But the outlook behind his clueless athleticism was elegantly summarized by the philosopher René Descartes.

In his *Meditations on First Philosophy*, Descartes argued that the mind and the body are two different substances. A substance, for philosophers, usually means something fundamental: the basic 'stuff' of the world. Humans, said Descartes, are made of two different kinds of stuff: thinking things and material things. Because of this, mind and body are barely part of the same world. They are coordinated, said Descartes, at the pineal gland. (Why? Partly because no one knew quite what the pineal gland did.)

This is what philosophers call 'substance dualism', and it is one of the most popular ideas in Western history. It says that the world, including humans, is basically divided. Even if mind and body are somehow joined in everyday life (which Descartes recognized), they are actually worlds apart.

Dualism usually brings with it a pecking order: mind at the top, and the flesh at the bottom. Descartes wanted certainty, for example, but was suspicious of bodily senses. He recognized that truth required *some* intimacy with the physical world, but he was wary of sight, touch, smell. In the *Meditations*, Descartes did away with every-thing he thought vague, until he was left with only the most certain thing: mind. 'Thinking is another attribute of the soul,' he wrote, 'and here I discover what belongs properly to myself. This alone is inseparable from me.' This is why he said, famously, 'I think, there-fore I am': only the mind was the *real* Descartes. The rest was dodgy, dubious flesh.

This is an old idea with a fine philosophical pedigree: the Greek philosopher Plato also believed that his mind was his 'true self'. Socrates, in Plato's *Phaedo*, described the body as 'heavy, oppressive, earthly, and visible', as opposed to the light, liberating, heavenly, invisible soul. But for Plato, and for the Christian churches who carried on his ideas, Descartes's suspicion was joined by contempt. The body caused errors of fact, but it also waylaid the good soul. The flesh goaded the spirit to be greedy, capricious and lustful – 'tainted and impure,' as Plato put it.

The body is, at its best, foreign to the mind – at its worst, corrupting of it.

These Boots are Made for Accelerators

Where does dualism come from? Well, not straight from philoso-phers. Thinkers like Plato and Descartes tweaked the ideas, but they had ordinary human origins – and still do.

For example, dualism is partly born of social and economic circumstances. In the Western world, white-collar work is the most common occupation. Professionals, 'knowledge workers' and low-paid service-sector employees have one thing in common: like me, they spend most of the day talking, reading and typing, and doing very little manual labour.

This would be fine if transport were a workout. But most workers drive, or are driven, to the office, in private cars or public transport. And over the last few decades, this has worsened: we are now walking less than ever before. And this is true for grocery shopping and other daily errands: the feet hit more accelerator and brake pedals than paths. While cycling is a boom sport worldwide, it is not yet mainstream as transport: bicycle trips represent only a tiny percentage of the world's daily trips. Forget biking to the office – many fans prefer to watch broadcasts of *others* cycling up hills in Porto-Vecchio.

The overall impression is of a civilization of 'mind workers', for whom walking is a brief transition from home to car, car park to office, car to shops – often while tapping screens and buttons, and taking calls. We grow accustomed to a professional life in which labour – and often identity – is chiefly mental not physical, and interaction virtual. We still have bodies, of course, but their contribution to character is diminished. In short, we live *seemingly* disembodied lives. This does not necessarily cause dualism, but it certainly promotes it, and is promoted by it.

Plato's and Descartes's wariness of the body also makes a lot of sense, even today. For all our medical advances, we are still fragile, fickle creatures, whose lives begin and end with pain and weakness. 'The proper form of address between man and man ought to be,' wrote Arthur Schopenhauer, 'not . . . *sir*, but *fellow sufferer*.' And our better motives are easily undone by hunger, sexual desire and illness. We can promise to jog weekly but slump on the couch instead, can try to stick to lean meats and steamed vegetables but get stuck into bowls of heaped pasta and glasses of Syrah. The mind, with its clear ideals and visions of happiness, seems foreign to viscera and hormones – compromised by strange association.

We Are Bodies

But this is no argument for dualism. The mistake made by Descartes, Plato and their kindred thinkers today, is to blame the body for our flaws, as if the flesh might be carved away from an otherwise pure mind. Others take the opposite position: they blame the mind for making the body weak or uncoordinated – for being 'off in the clouds', as if the flesh could work robotically without a psyche. Yet both dualisms are false: there is no 'thinking substance', and thinking is not something we do 'in our mind', as if this happened away from the body.

The philosopher Gilbert Ryle, in *The Concept of Mind*, noted that this is basically a dodgy metaphor: we see thinking as a kind of private conversation with ourselves. We believe that thoughts are words that are silently spoken 'in here', and then translated into public words with the throat, tongue and lips, or fingertips.

This portrait, said Ryle, is flawed. For example, speaking is itself a way of thinking – many ideas are better developed in company. Take a rambling chat while jogging together on a footpath or treadmill. We are not thinking 'in our minds' then turning this into speech: the conversation *is* the ideas – they are public, and developed together, amidst footfalls and breaths.

In fact, we often think with our whole body: gesticulating, counting on our fingers, pacing up and down in a room. As we will see with Charles Darwin, some ideas are better thought on foot than at a desk. If Descartes had worked while walking, instead of philosophizing for hours in bed, his meditations might have been less bloodless. ('Only thoughts conceived while walking,' wrote philosopher Friedrich Nietzsche with his usual bravado, 'have any value.')

Our language is fleshy too. Many of our everyday metaphors have to do with common human physiology. For example, we might speak of a sprinter 'rising' in the ranks, or a footballer's career going 'backwards'. But these athletes are not literally ascending or reversing. These are metaphors that require a grasp of bodily reality: how it feels to walk up a steep hill, or fall behind in a schoolyard sprint. (Think, too, of how I just used 'grasp'.) Philosophers easily forget this. When Descartes wrote of 'carrying out' the work of his *Meditations*, for example, he was nodding to the strain of lifting a weight: something baffling to anything other than a mind in a body, heavy in a world of matter and gravity.

Feelings are also embodied. Think of 1980s tennis bad boy John McEnroe. His court tantrums were not simply signs of some inner anger – symbols of invisible emotion. His rage suffused his grimacing face, clenched fists and the arc of his arms smashing the racquet. French philosopher Maurice Merleau-Ponty, who took issue with Descartes's ideas, made this point in *The World of Perception*. 'Where is this anger? People will say that it is in the mind of my interlocutor. What this means is not entirely clear,' he wrote. 'None of this takes place in some otherworldly realm, located beyond the body of the angry man.' The anger, says Merleau-Ponty,

Dualism? You cannot be serious.

is 'bound up' with the body, and the same is true of joy, diffidence, pride and humility.

So Descartes was wrong. We are not minds who *have* bodies, in the way we have a cricket bat or pair of sneakers. We *are* bodies. 'Body am I entirely, and nothing more,' wrote Nietzsche in *Thus Spoke Zarathustra*, 'and soul is only the name of something in the body.' Thinking and feeling always happen in, with and through the flesh.

The point is not that we all need to quit reading Descartes's *Meditations*. The philosopher simply neatened up a very old, common belief. The point is how easily even the greatest minds can become alienated from their flesh. Descartes was so used to his body, he forgot how much of his mind was embodied.

This happens regularly today: physical life and mental life can become easily divorced. And the separated parties are not always on speaking terms. Exercise is something done with one's body. It is public and physical. Thinking is something done with one's mind. It is private and ethereal. As the Chad stereotype suggests, it can seem normal for neither to benefit from the other.

Chad, Meet Heidegger

But so what? How important is philosophy when going for a run or lifting weights at the local gym?

Well, to begin, dualism gives us an excuse for *not* exercising. Because the fitness and sports industry is seen as a colony run by Chads, physical exertion can seem foreign and, quite frankly, a bit smug. We see grimacing under a bench press, or sweating along the footpath, as torture for narcissists, too addicted to bodily beauty to read or think. Professional sports stars, with their glib sound-bites and off-field clowning, make this prejudice worse: physical effort seems the province of vain fools. In other words, dualism does not straight-forwardly cause laziness, but it can kill off ambition: we become more likely to tolerate a partial life, in which we push our intellects but not our quadriceps or lungs. We congratulate ourselves for our distance from the flesh and its supposed frailties, like pride or conceit.

For professionals and other middle-class 'mental workers', a completely sedentary lifestyle is actually quite rare. This is partly because of public health campaigns. For the past thirty years, we have been told – by advertisers, schools, doctors and government depart-ments – that we need exercise for our organs to work well. We are quoted statistics on obesity and heart disease. Being morbidly over-weight, for example, increases the chances of diabetes, heart attacks and strokes, and is associated with stillbirths in obese mothers-to-be. Research consistently finds that just sitting, regardless of whether we are fat or thin, can kill.

To overcome this sedentary lifestyle, many turn to the gym, particularly amongst the middle classes. (Participation in sports and exercise rises with education and income.) And rightly so. But this is not without its problems. To begin, it encourages the idea that mental and physical work are somehow at odds: different worlds, with different uniforms and music. In the office, I work with my mind; in Fitness First, with my body. As I step into the gymnasium, I am one of the Chads.

More philosophically, exercising because of illness or injury – or the threat of each – can also encourage dualism. This is because our bodies become what Martin Heidegger, the twentieth-century German philosopher, called 'present-at-hand'.

In *Being and Time*, Heidegger observed that many of our tools are invisible to us. We do not notice the racquet as we hit the ball, for example. He called this 'ready-to-hand'. When ready-to-hand, the tool is no longer a thing on its own. Instead, it is intertwined with us – with our purposes and practices, motives and expectations.

Heidegger argued that when a tool fails, it becomes visible again: we peer at the racquet and wonder why the ball is bouncing oddly. We check the strings and handle-tape. The tool is now more present-at-hand: we suddenly see the racquet as a thing apart from us, and the rest of the world. It is still a tool, of course, but it has lost its invisible intertwining. Heidegger called this the 'conspicuousness of the unusable'.

Now, our hands, legs and lungs are not tools, but they are often invisible in the same way, until something goes wrong: heart palpitations, breathlessness or chafing from thickened thighs. A doctor's diagnosis can do the same thing: make our bodies or lifestyles somehow conspicuous, to use Heidegger's word. When we turn to the gym, garage weights or running track to improve our health, we can treat our bodies as if they were present-at-hand tools: malfunctioning equipment that requires tinkering.

It certainly is true that we might need stronger muscles, denser bones and more efficient lungs – nobody need deny the medical value of fitness. But exercising *only* for health can worsen the very dualism that led to a sedentary lifestyle in the first place; we behave as if we were minds servicing bodies, like a sports repairman fixing a racquet. The Chad ideal adds to this: the personal trainer is like the repairman, giving the customer technical tips for tightening strings.

This can be harmless over a few weeks or months: we lose some weight, gain a little muscle or increase our lung capacity. But once the obvious ailments are gone, we often stop exercising altogether – the machine is fixed, so to speak. This is partly why so many gym memberships go unused. Not always because we are lazy or forgetful, but because the fear of illness or injury has gone, and our limbs and organs are again invisible. Dualism can encourage fitful or capricious exercise – if it encourages it at all.

Descartes: Fitness Killjoy

Dualism can also dumb exercise down, so that we miss its intellectual and physical rewards. As we will see, workouts can be intellectually pleasurable or ethically challenging. They can change our thinking, and be changed by our thinking.

Because of this, measuring bicep inches, or checking the run counter for a 'personal best', can actually stop us exercising. The novelty of mechanical tweaking only lasts so long. We get bored, anaesthetized or simply cannot justify the pain. The problem is not that we are striving. The problem is that we are doing so narrowly: without an eye for our whole humanity. And this is not enough to keep us challenged and curious in the long run (or the short swim). The gym membership lapses, or the brand-new sit-up machine gets dusty.

Growing More Greek

For inspiration on how to avoid dualism, and bring our minds and bodies into play together, it helps to turn back to the ancient Greeks. Nietzsche called the Greeks the 'highest type of man', and hoped that modern scholarship might one day take up their example. But their example was not just academic. 'We are growing more Greek by the day; at first . . . in concepts and evaluations,' he wrote in his 1885 diary, 'but one day, let us hope, also in our bodies!'

What attracted Nietzsche to the Greeks was partly their celebration of physicality. The perfect human being was not torn between frail flesh and eternal spirit. He or she was a living whole, whose mind and body worked *happily* together. 'Can one go more dangerously wrong,' he wrote in his notebook in 1888, 'than by despising the body? As if that contempt did not condemn all intellectuality to sickliness'.

The Greek outlook was summed up succinctly by the Athenian general, historian and memoirist Xenophon. As a young man, Xenophon was one of Socrates' followers. In his memoirs, written in the fourth century before Christ, Xenophon recollected Socrates chastising a lazy companion, Epigenes – not just for his ideas, but for his sloth, and its corruption of character and thought.

'You're out of training,' Socrates comments to Epigenes one afternoon. The youth replies casually that he does not exercise. (He is the anti-Chad: mind without muscle.) Socrates will have none of it. The old philosopher first notes the importance of fitness for war. Soldiers are killed because they are flabby and easily knackered; or captured, then enslaved or ransomed. Fit Athenians, says Socrates, 'live out

Socrates and pupil Alcibiades.
'It is a base thing for a man to wax old in careless self-neglect . . .'

their lives with greater pleasure and distinction, and leave behind them a better start for their children.'

But fitness is more than a military duty, says Socrates. It makes the body fitter for *any* challenge. 'You can take it from me,' he tells Epigenes, 'there is no other feat of endurance . . . in which you will be at a disadvantage'. Tellingly, Socrates is not only talking about sport, labour or war. For Socrates, philosophy too is promoted by exercise. 'Many people's minds are so invaded by forgetfulness, despondency, irritability and insanity because of their poor physical condition,' Socrates argues, 'that their knowledge is actually driven out of them.'

Having revealed the martial and intellectual value of exercise, Xenophon concludes with a typically Greek message: we only have one life, and youth is brief. To be healthy without trying to run faster and longer, or harden one's muscles, is to squander a chance to be *more* than one is; to miss the unique joy of striving, however painful. In Benjamin Jowett's translation, Socrates' sporty lyricism is clear:

It is a base thing for a man to wax old in careless self-neglect before he has lifted up his eyes and seen what manner of man he was made to be, in the full perfection of bodily strength and beauty. But these glories are withheld from him who is guilty of self-neglect, for they are not wont to blaze forth unbidden.

The point is this: exercise was not just a dull duty for the classical Greeks. Yes, citizen soldiers had to be fit, and no doubt many wearied of the daily oiling and grappling, grunting and lifting. But, from nobles like Xenophon to commoners like Socrates, the Greeks often saw exercise as a way to savour their full humanity. It was *theirs*, not Chad's; not owned by a professional athlete or trainer. They kept sprinting, wrestling and throwing their javelins, not just because of war or health, but because it polished their souls, and they got a buzz out of it.

Put more precisely, this is the Greek message: exercise offers virtues and pleasures, alongside hard bodies.

Becoming Ethically Buffed

What does this mean, practically? The word 'virtue' has an old-fashioned stuffiness to it nowadays; a scent of dust and mothballs. But virtue is not just a vague synonym for conservative morality or sexual prudery. Virtue is the English translation of the Greek *arête*, or 'excellence'.

This idea of virtue is helpful for us today because it is neither a purely cognitive nor purely physiological portrait of ethics. It involves the whole human being.

Aristotle, in his *Nicomachean Ethics*, argued that virtues are not just concepts. He mocked theorizers who talked about ethics without actually *doing* ethics – like a patient who listens carefully to a doctor's diagnosis, then ignores all her prescriptions. 'Neither by nature . . . nor contrary to nature do the virtues arise in us,' Aristotle wrote, 'rather we are adapted by nature to receive them, and are made perfect by habit.' In short: virtue comes from habit, not just gabbing about goodness.

But habit is not enough on its own. Virtue also involves desire: when we are morally excellent, this is more than reflex. We *want* to be good, said Aristotle, and we get pleasure out of achieving this.

Virtue also involves choice: we cannot be blamed for our vices if we have no say in our own excellence. 'No one blames those who are ugly by nature, we blame those who are so owing to want of exercise and care,' Aristotle noted. 'So it is, too, with respect to weakness and infirmity.' In other words, virtue involves reasonable decision-making. The tantrum-throwing tennis player is frowned upon because we know he is an adult, who can do better.

Reason is also important for the virtues themselves, which Aristotle saw as means between extremes. For example, courage is a mean between cowardice and foolhardiness. (Chad, for the record, is foolhardy. This is why he gets shot. In a cupboard.) The courageous rugby player will neither flee, screaming, from a tackle, nor walk slowly into a pack of giant defenders. He will judge the danger, and dodge and weave as his duty demands. Put another way, he will behave reasonably, with an eye for the game, his goals (literal and figurative), and how to win without being crippled.

This combination of habit, desire and free rationality is why Aristotle called virtue a 'state of character'. In other words, it is a disposition, which is neither solely mental nor solely physical. It requires action, desire, thought and will. Pulling it all together is what Aristotle called *phronesis*, or 'practical wisdom'. (The Latin was *prudentia*: prudence.) *Phronesis* is the knack that comes from thoughtful practice in varied circumstances. In this, it is a typically Greek kind of knowledge: learned as much with one's hands and feet as with one's intellect.

This ideal is why the Greeks were so keen on exercise in education: it developed virtues alongside muscles. And they were generous about this: they recognized the morality of dance, for example, alongside sport and military training. In Xenophon's 'Dinner Party',

Socrates praises a dancer somersaulting over swords: her gymnastics have taught her courage. Even Plato, with his radical dualism, agreed with this. His ideal city, described in the late dialogue *Laws*, included martial arts, games and dance training for the citizens. Like Aristotle and Xenophon, he typified the Greek ideal: strive physically and mindfully, and enjoy the rewards. ('Platon', for the record, was his wrestling nickname.)

In this, the Greeks were quite farsighted. As we will see, jogging or climbing, for example, can develop virtues like consistency and humility. We are rediscovering what many Greeks took for granted: exercise is a chance to educate our bodies *and* minds, at once.

This focus on virtue provides a morale boost for geeks (like me) in the gym, wondering why we are plodding on the treadmill and trying to bench our own bodyweight. But, more importantly, it also provides a lasting motivation for everyone interested in fitness. We play tennis or football, visit the swimming pool or running track, not just to become beautiful, or push away the spectre of death. Over the months and years, we can become more aware of subtle changes to character: we are more proud, humble, generous or constant. This is the Greek lesson: what we get out of the gym is more than a buffed body – it is a more defined version of ourselves. And this is a lifelong project, not just a summer fad.

The Joys of Wholeness

But exercise is not all moral improvement. It also gives us a buzz. Yes, being good, as Aristotle argued, can be satisfying in itself. But there are more subtle kinds of pleasure involved in sports and games.

As is suggested by Xenophon's 'full perfection of bodily strength and beauty', there is an existential joy to workouts, which celebrates the whole human being.

The moods of exercise can also give pleasure. From ordinary strolls to mountain climbing, fitness can have a psychological payoff: reverie or a clearer identity, for example. In each case, these rewards come from the to and fro between mind and body.

This is vital for lifelong fitness, because we can enjoy exercise even when we fail, lose, or cannot see improvements in muscle tone or lung capacity. We can do yoga, for example, for the bliss encouraged by its stretching and meditation – even if we cannot become the supple knots we see in photos. We can do karate to savour painful freedom, even if we are regularly knocked in the snout. By remembering the workout's mental pleasures, we give ourselves more reasons to stop by the gym, put on the compression tights and sneakers, or don the togs or white pyjamas.

So exercising intelligently does not have to mean researching supplements or buying the latest pulse monitor. It certainly does not mean applauding Chad's dim muscularity. It means overcoming dualism, and getting the most out of every step, push, stroke, reach and kick – and keeping on enjoying these, even as our ligaments become more brittle, or our lungs more weak. Intelligent exercise is a commitment to wholeness: enhancing and enjoying our full humanity, while we can.

In this spirit, this book is not a 'how to' manual for exercise. It will not provide tips for correct kettle-bell swings or jogging heel alignment. It is an introduction to the psychological rewards, and ethical virtues, of fitness; a companion to exercise, which shows how our minds can thrive as we sweat and strain – how our muscles swell and flex with the right mindset.

1. Reverie

Charles Darwin. The world's greatest naturalist. Collector of barnacles, orchids and beetles. Jane Austen fan. Stalker of foxes. And a dogged walker.

Darwin's daily strolls played an important role in his life, but also in the development of his ideas. They reveal the unique intellectual value of reverie in exercise: reorganizing concepts and revitalizing perception.

Sandwalk

We find Darwin on an ordinary day at Down House, in Kent. He is walking on a sandy path, fidgeting with his fingers. His stick beats a slow rhythm on the stones. His company: a white fox terrier, Polly. She pants a little, as does he. The path is edged with oaks, many covered with moss. They creak a little, as does he. The stooping stroller is enjoying his 'thinking path': the Sandwalk, a wonky rectangular track around a copse of hazel, birch, dogwood, privet and holly. Every now and then, he kicks one of the flint pebbles piled by the path: a record of another turn.

Charles Darwin was not a Romantic prophet or visionary, knocking back higher truths with absinthe. He was an inspired

The Sandwalk: Darwin's 'thinking path'.

workhorse: curious, lucid, patient. And, just as importantly, Darwin was a man of unchanging routines. 'My life goes on like clockwork,' he wrote in 1846 to Robert FitzRoy, captain of the famous HMS *Beagle*, 'and I am fixed on the spot where I shall end it.' Every day, the Darwin household saw the same rhythms of work, recreation and correspondence. And every day, between his tens of thousands of barnacles ('I hate a barnacle as no man ever did before') and even more letters, Darwin walked. He rose early, and took a turn around the Sandwalk. And he did the same at noon, enjoying 'a very little walk in an idle frame of mind', then returning for lunch and study.

Even with Darwin's sedentary career of crustaceans and correspondence, he walked far more than many today. And he did so despite regular ill health, sometimes ending in violent nausea – the symptoms, perhaps, of a parasite infection from an assassin-bug bite in Argentina, or a less exotic (but more common) digestive illness, like diverticulitis. Trekking abroad and, later, researching with equal drive, Darwin was hardly a retiring consumptive. But his health was poor, and often worsened by stress. Yet even in his sixties, Darwin kept walking every day, in sunshine or 'heavy rain', as he put it, with some understatement.

Walking was, for Darwin, a lifelong exercise – somewhere between a hobby and a mania. In his autobiography, he noted that he was known for his long strolls, even as a child. 'I had, as a very young boy,' he wrote, 'a strong taste for solitary walks.' For the budding naturalist, the point was not simply to get from home to school, but to reflect without interruption. One afternoon, returning along Shrewsbury's old fortifications, he fell seven or eight feet – he had not seen that the parapet was gone. 'I often became quite absorbed,' he wrote simply. Later, as a young man in 1826, Darwin went on a walking tour of North Wales with friends, hiking some thirty miles a day with knapsacks on their backs.

Darwin's health eventually stopped him climbing mountains – his last geological trip, to observe glacial landscapes in Wales, was when he was in his early thirties. But he kept walking right until the end. His son Francis recalled his father in the last weeks of his life, suffering a painful seizure: the old man was walking at the time. Note Francis's emphasis: 'he got home with difficulty, and this was the last time that he was able to reach his favourite "Sand-walk".' For Darwin, to forgo his stroll around the copse was no trivial thing.

Question: Darwin often walked a mile or two every day, not including stairs and pacing from nerves. How far did you walk today?

Walker's Reverie

Why was walking so important for Darwin? It was not simply for fitness, though he shared the Victorian enthusiasm for a 'constitutional'. It was not out of paternal contempt for the noise of family life – on the contrary, he was a warm and playful father. It was not just Darwin's love of nature, though this was clearly an ongoing passion – witness his disdain for London, a 'vile, smoky place, where a man loses a great part of the best enjoyments of life.' And it was not simply to burn off the snuff he sniffed daily. (Without the drug, he was 'lethargic, stupid, and melancholy,' he complained to his friend, the botanist J. D. Hooker.)

Darwin's walks were also an exercise in reflection – a kind of moving meditation. This enriched his scientific work, and gratified his constant curiosity. Walks, wrote his plain-speaking son, were for Darwin's 'hard thinking'.

Francis's phrasing gives the impression of plodding abstraction, but Darwin's description of 'an idle frame of mind' on walks suggests something more creative. Neuroscientists have argued that exercise can encourage innovation and problem-solving. Not because it helps us study more rigorously, but because it allows our intellect to relax a little; to digest our meal of facts and arguments. Researchers describe it as 'transient hypofrontality': the prefrontal cortex, which helps to make general concepts and rules, is turned down, while the motor and sensory parts of the brain are turned up. It's what might be called 'walker's reverie'. Busy with pounding legs and pumping arms, the intellect's walls come down, and previously parted ideas and impressions can freely mingle – what neuropsychologist and novelist Kylie Ladd calls 'the free flow of novel, unfiltered ideas and impulses.' Exactly what a trailblazing scientist needed in order to develop a new theory of species marked by constant, purposeless change.

Walking the Dogma

The word 'species', now so tied to Darwin's name, is itself a clue to the intellectual importance of reverie. For most Victorians, the word suggested something perfect and eternal. It was a Latin translation of the Greek *eidos*: idea, pattern, form. For Plato, forms were the true reality, more real than physical stuff. Like Plato, Aristotle saw the forms as unchanging, unmoving: what continued amongst the world's flux and diversity. The species of life were the ultimate proof of this: generations were born and died, but the forms of molluscs, foxes and men stayed the same.

The species also had what the Greeks called a *telos*: a final end. Every *eidos* had some ultimate goal, aim, purpose. These ideas were taken up by Christian thinkers, and influenced many in the West right up to the nineteenth century. American philosopher John Dewey, in a 1909 talk on Darwin, described this common outlook:

> From the casual drift of daily weather, through the uneven recurrence of seasons and unequal return of seed time and harvest, up to the majestic sweep of the heavens . . . and from this to the unchanging pure and contemplative intelligence beyond nature lies one unbroken fulfilment of ends.

Put simply, before Darwin, to say 'species' was to name something obvious, pure, perfect and eternal. This was taken for granted in school textbooks, church sermons and polite conversation. Over the centuries, the idea of unchanging nature had itself become unchanging: a legacy of habit, institutions including the Vatican and the Church of England, and the dogma of revealed truth.

Like a handful of thinkers before and alongside him, Darwin gradually began to believe otherwise. He was by no means absolutely certain of his theory – his confidence grew slowly. Witness his quietly doubting note in July 1837, above his sketch of an evolutionary tree: 'I think'. Anxious about his radical ideas, Darwin began to suffer heart palpitations around this time – the theory was a challenge, not only to the public, but to Darwin himself. He was 'almost convinced' of evolution, he wrote to a friend in 1844, but it was 'like confessing to a murder,' he added. Part of Darwin had not given up on the old worldview.

Reverie during exercise allowed Darwin to shake up these received ideas, to undo the false certainty of perfection, which had held on for over twenty centuries. Obviously this required painstaking research and careful argument – one cannot simply take a turn and overthrow two millennia of doctrine. But, in combination with intellectual rigour and curiosity, Darwin's Sandwalk stroll was an opportunity to resist mental rigidity – to stretch and make supple his psychological muscles. His biographer Janet Browne wrote that this walk was 'the private source of his conviction that his theory was true.'

Not everyone has Darwin's fondness for rain-drenched meandering; not everyone has a rambling rural path to comfortably stroll on – snow and gales or midsummer heat can rule out reverie. But, as with jogging, a spell on the treadmill is certainly better than nothing. Poet David Morley, whose poems often arise from hikes, strolls, swims and climbs, puts it neatly. 'William Wordsworth composed poems while pacing the metres of his garden's gravel path,' he writes. '*Solvitur ambulando* – it is solved by walking.' If Wordsworth can poeticize while walking to and fro in a yard, we can certainly enjoy reverie on a treadmill or footpath. The important thing is to work the hypofrontality into professional and domestic timetables: better a stationary stroll in a nearby gymnasium or your own garage than more sitting. Those in the city can also take stairs instead of lifts: not only a harder workout, but also a good opportunity for undistracted solitude.

Tip: *If you are stuck on a problem, try a walk instead of a coffee or tea break. A stroll can be more relaxing, and more helpful, than sitting still.*

Animal Alertness

Why walking and not another exercise? With the exception of jogging, most sports require too much tactical calculation. Reverie arises partly because the exertion is dull, requiring a little sweat but no brains. Darwin recognized this himself. Horse riding, which he adored, was not quite banal enough to augment his mood. 'He would say that riding prevented him thinking much more effectually than walking,' wrote Francis, 'that having to attend to the horse gave him occupation sufficient to prevent any really hard thinking.' Darwin's placid gelding, Tommy, was an antidote to thinking, full stop. Whereas walking around his Sandwalk was a way of thinking things anew.

Likewise for running. While jogging was not, for Victorians like Darwin, a familiar exercise, it is now a regular source of reverie for millions. For example, in *What I Talk About When I Talk About Running*, author and regular marathon runner Haruki Murakami (whom we will meet later) describes his psychological 'void':

> I run in order to acquire a void. But as you might expect, the occasional stray thought will slip into this void. People's minds can't be a complete blank. Human beings are not strong or consistent enough to sustain a vacuum. What I mean is, the kinds of thoughts and ideas that invade my emotions as I run remain subordinate to that void. Lacking

Riding on Tommy: Darwin replaces his thinking cap.

content, they are just random thoughts that gather around that void.

This is a classic description of transient hyperfrontality: a private, moving daydream, which keeps Murakami calmer, and more creative.

Walking and jogging also work at a more contemplative speed, and allow us to meditate on our surroundings. Horse riding let Darwin get quickly from place to place: from the anchored HMS *Beagle* to an inland jungle, or (not quite so quickly, on Tommy) from Down House to nearby Kentish valley views. And, just like a bike or car, it was exhilarating or calming, depending on the mount. But when Darwin wanted to stop and take notice, he walked. Witness his boffin's joy on the island of Santiago, off the coast of Africa:

> Nobody but a person fond of Natural History can imagine the pleasure of strolling under cocoa-nuts in a thicket of bananas and coffee-plants, and an endless number of wild flowers. And this island, that has given me so much instruction and delight, is reckoned the most uninteresting place that we perhaps shall touch.

As this suggests, reverie can have an immediacy to it, which is rewarding. This too is a Darwinian point: we are creatures evolved in and with environments, and our senses and motor skills are most alive in interplay with a tactile, vibrant world. We act upon this world, and it upon us; we seek and find fulfilment in these rhythms of to and fro. To involve ourselves, bodily, in a varied and varying situation is to augment our existence a little. In this way, wrote Dewey, 'the designs of living are widened and enriched. Fulfillment is more massive and more subtly shaded.'

This animal alertness was something Darwin had in common with the life he famously studied. 'I remember him gently touching a flower he delighted in,' wrote Francis, 'it was the same simple admiration a child might have.' On the Sandwalk, young squirrels ran up his back, their mum yelping from a tree. He picked up beetles (another favourite) crawling across the path; saw a sleeping fox in the 'Big-Woods', which stared at Darwin, baffled, before it ran off. This was more than entertainment for the naturalist: it was intimate familiarity with a varied and changing world, what Dewey called 'the multiplicity of doings and undergoings'. Reverie thrives in a dynamic environment, slowly appreciated.

The point is not that every exercise must be a bucolic adventure – we city sorts, in 'vile, smoky places', have feet too. The point is that exercise can do more than encourage a mood of creativity. It can also give us something to be creative *about*. It combines reverie with intimate stimulation, and the pace to best savour it.

For example, anyone taking a long walk around their neighbourhood, after years behind the wheel, will be surprised by the quirks normally missed at rush hour. From today's school drop-off and pickup: a still dragonfly, sunning itself on a pear tree; lines of ants, marching along a suburban kerb and massing on a cherry tree outside a wool shop; the rounded geometry of a spider's web, putting a clothes line to shame.

We cannot enjoy this reverie properly if we are hunched over the handlebars, let alone travelling at fifty miles an hour behind safety glass, fiddling with the climate control. Better to savour the opportunity for gentle congress with a surprising world.

Drive and you miss it: very local architecture.

Tip: Take a walk around your neighbourhood, school or workplace, and try to find at least three surprising features. For example: novel architecture, botanical oddities or geographical puzzles.

Solitude

Do we have to exercise alone for reverie? Darwin was certainly no misanthrope – witness his pleasure in strolls with Emma, when her 'strength and weather allowed'. He also combined walking with scientific conversation. Some of the dons at Cambridge called him 'the man who walks with Henslow', after the professor with whom he strolled. Exercise, in other words, need not be antisocial.

Still, solitude is a vital part of reverie, at least when walking or jogging outdoors. To really savour the combination of reverie and stimulation, we have to avoid distractions: even those of good company.

And far more disrupting than face-to-face sociability is something foreign to Darwin: modern telecommunications and entertainment technology. Nowadays, many pedestrians are struck by what researchers call 'inattentional blindness'. Plugged into iPods, or pecking phones and tablets, our eyes and ears are working perfectly, but we do not necessarily see and hear what is right in front of us. Inattentional blindness can be dangerous: witness the rapid increase of pedestrian deaths recently documented in the United States. Of those victims wearing headphones, most were hit by trains. The mechanisms are not yet fully understood by neuroscientists, but distraction is certainly central to this myopia: the stimuli are received

The gentle art of not-noticing.

and processed by the brain, yet the conscious mind is busy with Twitter or Tinie Tempah.

This is not a cause for moral panic or Luddite lamentation, but for a certain mindfulness. However regularly we glance up the footpath and road, divided attention has large holes in it: big enough for a train to slip through. Spider webs, blue lobelia and other quotidian curiosities do not stand a chance.

Tip: try walking without headphones, and with your phone off, or at least in your bag or pocket. If you unwittingly fiddle and paw at your phone, as I do, resist the reflex to take it out.

Having said this, treadmill walkers, snatching a stroll during lunch or after the kids are in bed, might actually benefit from headphones. While it can be rewarding to meditate quietly, reverie thrives on a little stimulation. Tactile feedback is obviously minimal on a treadmill, but music, audiobooks and podcasts can make the session more evocative and provocative. (And there are no trains to worry about.)

A Holiday on Foot

The point is to be mindful of the benefits of gentle exercise; to remember that we are doing more than tightening our thighs and calves. We are also loosening our minds, and giving them interesting things to contemplate in this state. In this, exercise can be a break from our customary narrowness. If we are not all Charles Darwin, we still have our own barnacles: duties that require ongoing, rigid thought and planning. Spreadsheet calculations, examination cramming, sales targets or the logistics of household management. What we are often lacking is not focus, but the mental ease that reverie provides: the chance to undo our usual intellectual rigidity, and allow our minds to seek novelty. In other words, exercise can be a habit that undoes habit: a way to regularly shake up our intellectual routines.

So Darwin's walks are a reminder of the joy of exercises like walking and jogging, but also of the discipline and effort required to do them well; to allow these commonplace exertions do their psychological work. Reverie, in other words, is an achievement, not a gift. Undertaken without distraction, these ordinary exercises can actually be exceptional: daily holidays from false certainty and anaesthesia.

2. Pride

Sprinting is one of the world's most popular sports and has been since the ancient Greeks dashed around stadiums (sometimes in full armour). And the Greeks were unashamedly proud of their victories – often to the point of boastfulness.

This pride remains a vital part of committed exercise. It is not simply conceit or arrogance, but a pleasure in our own existence. In this, it is also a sign of existential responsibility: a drive to define ourselves more ardently before youth and life leave us.

Freedom and Nausea

It is an ordinary spring afternoon: fickle blue skies and copious pollen. I am at the foot of an ordinary suburban hill, next to red-brick retirees' apartments with massed pelargoniums. Most of my neighbours are watching television, or in their offices, perhaps grabbing a takeaway coffee for the drive home.

My day, so far, has been equally ordinary. Transcribing edits for this book, I looked like a stock photo in a news story on modern sedentary ailments: typing at the laptop, my bum sinking ever lower into the faded bridge chair. At one point, it felt as if my lower back and the chair had become one: a grand union of the kind praised by mystics and rightly condemned by physiotherapists. Business as usual for a thirty-something professional.

But I am about to do something unusual: hill sprints. Despite my congested sinuses and the obvious fact of gravity, I will run up this hill, as fast as I can. I will then jog back down to the foot. Having pulled up my torn, sagging compression tights, I will then do it all again: fourteen times.

The sprints are, quite frankly, a buzz. After the day's intellectual labour, they suggest freedom: the impression of reaching out and up, past myself, to the hill's apex. Each burst feels like potential energy realized: not just calories converted into work, but all my morning's restlessness transformed into a single unchecked, uncomplicated movement.

In *Born to Run*, Australian Olympian sprinter Cathy Freeman describes this as being 'happy and free' – even after ten laps of an old sawdust track, the young Freeman was 'safe and strong, like [she] was the only person in the world.' And running has no monopoly on this. Champion cyclist Cadel Evans, in *Close to Flying*, writes of 'riding for the love of it'. 'You float . . . drift . . . sweep,' he says, like flying. Again: a feeling of being liberated from ordinary concerns, of being above the usual guff.

Much of adult life requires a quantum of caution or care – the need censor words, restrain aggressive urges. My hill sprints are the antithesis of this: they have a purity to them – a simple, single-minded dedication, which refuses second-guessing and delicacy.

Tip: Run as fast as you can, for as long as you can. If you do this already, try it up a hill. Try to enjoy the simplicity of it.

Hill sprints: give me liberty or give me breath.

The point is not that running is an easy craft. On the contrary, it requires serious concentration on technique: footfall, stride, balance, rhythm. The point is that, as with cycling downhill or pushing weights, once I have committed to the exertion, it has an emancipating simplicity to it. This is *me*, unimpeded by the chair's mahogany arms and my own moderating anxiety.

Confession: before a couple of years ago, the last time I ran as fast as possible was the early 1980s: my childhood.

As the sets add up, I slow down. I push myself to run as fast as possible, but my 'possible' is more sluggish and breathy. Sprinting has become running has become jogging. By the fifteenth sprint, my body is numb from impact on the concrete, and my heart has a drum 'n' bass cadence to it. The feeling of liberty has vanished, and what remains is plodding, slightly desperate stubbornness, and then retching disorientation.

I do not feel free. I feel sick.

But alongside my drained nausea is pleasure. It begins once the exercise is done, and continues well after the queasiness and fatigue have gone.

It is similar to the satisfaction I feel when running on an inclined treadmill, sprinting pell-mell on a stationary bike, or, with trembling quadriceps, combining kettle-bell squats with upright rows.

Importantly, this need not be enjoyed in spring sunshine. Australian writer and amateur power-lifter Clint Greagen writes about the 'raw animal-type thrill' he gets from evening workouts in his garage. Seeing the stacked bar bent over his back gives Greagen a buzz. 'It's very primal and a great change from the thinking part of myself,' he writes, 'which I'm stuck with the majority of every day.'

I enjoy this pleasure now, as I describe my puffing ascent: it is pride.

Pleasure in Oneself

What exactly is pride? To get to the bottom of this pleasure, we have to take a detour around Christian ideas. Pride was almost a four-letter word in the Christian West. 'Do not love the world or anything in the world,' says 1 John 2: 15–16. 'If anyone loves the world, love for the Father is not in them. For everything in the world – the lust of the flesh, the lust of the eyes, and the pride of life – comes not from the Father but from the world.'

There is an otherworldliness in this, which denies pleasure in general, and pleasure in oneself in particular. The more we get pleasure from ourselves, the less we attend to the Lord. In doing so, we make *ourselves* the source of beauty and joy, rather than the Godhead. This is why, for the Church fathers and theologians, pride was one of the chief sins: a love of oneself that turned away from God.

To avoid this, the Church recommended humility instead of pride – seeing ourselves as somewhat ugly. If we are born broken, then we need fixing: we will seek pleasure in God's grace instead of our own 'lust of the eyes'. No hill sprints for John the Evangelist.

A better source of wisdom on pride is the philosopher David Hume. He was not a sprinter or power-lifter. As his portrait suggests, he was not an avid exerciser at all – more a sedentary gourmand. But the great Enlightenment thinker gave a very helpful definition of pride, which avoids the Christian distaste for bodily gratification. It also fits with the ancient Greek pleasure in physical exertion, which we will turn to a little later.

Hume's definition of pride is a deceptively simple one: pleasure in oneself.

In his landmark *A Treatise of Human Nature*, Hume pointed out that pride actually has two parts: the cause of the pleasure, and the object we attribute it to. The cause is something like muscular legs, for example, or a heart that beats steadily and strongly. I get pleasure from these, because they suggest power, speed, robustness. These, in turn, promise *more* pleasure: of safety from threats, cardiovascular health, desirability to my wife, and so on. (In other words, we can also find pleasure in the promise of pleasure.) So pleasure is not random. It is based on what we value.

But how does this pleasure become pride in ourselves? This is why Hume introduced the idea of the object. With pride, the object is myself. I can never actually see or touch this 'self', but I do have an idea of it. And this idea is related to other ideas: 'my' legs, 'my' heart, for example. So the pleasure is passed along psychologically: from legs and heart to 'me'.

Hume noted that this pleasure is natural, but not everyone will feel pride in the same things. This gets back to value. We appreciate value by 'constitution . . . custom, or by caprice,' writes Hume. For example, we might agree that a leg is muscular, but not find this beautiful. It all hangs on the ties between ideas: muscular legs might make me feel more manly and desirable, or awkward, brutish and repugnant. Next to my sedentary friend's soft calves, my legs encourage pride; next to my weightlifting friend's striated quadriceps, they inspire humility.

David Hume: tights, yes; sprints, no.

And what is 'cute' to a spectator might be useless for an athlete. American Olympian Carmelita Jeter sees her naked body as beautiful: but for its strength and agility, not its petite prettiness. 'I'm not here to look cute,' she told ESPN. 'I'm out here to be powerful, be aggressive.' In short, there are no simple rules of pleasure.

This is why pride is often considered a virtue: because it shows that we value the right things. What is 'right' will change with age, geography, era – and profession, as Jeter's example suggests. But civilization works because we are taught as children not just to think about what's important, but also to *like* it; to find it pleasant or fulfilling.

Put simply, pride is sanctioned pleasure in something worthwhile, which we associate with ourselves.

Question: Stand naked in a mirror, and compare yourself mentally to someone less fit. Now compare yourself to a professional athlete. Use photos if you have to. Did your feelings change? How?

The Joy of a Firmer . . . 'I'

But what is valuable in exertion? For this, we can return to the ancient Greeks, who generally had no religious hang-ups about bodily beauty and strength. They were also happy to boast about their muscles and swiftness – pride was a virtue, not a sin. If we cannot all have their climate, we can still learn from their seemingly arrogant attitude: they reveal the existential value of pride.

At the Olympic games, held in Olympia every four years, the most prestigious contest was the pentathlon. Pentathletes vied in five events: long jump, discus, javelin, wrestling and the stadium sprint, which was about 220 yards. As with today's hundred-metre sprint, the sprint was the most prestigious competition. And it was not the only footrace. The Greeks also competed in a double sprint, a longer run of three miles, and another race in military armour, called the *hoplitodromos*.

Like today's Olympians, the ancient Olympic track stars received no prize money, but some were given pensions, free food (for life), parades, portraits in sculpture and over-the-top adulation. ('This is indeed a very wrong custom,' complained the sixth-century BC philosopher Xenophanes, 'nor is it right to prefer strength to excellent wisdom.')

As this suggests, the Greeks were not ashamed to praise and be praised, particularly when it came to running. Achilles, in Homer's eighth-century BC poem the *Iliad*, is regularly called 'swift runner'. His friend Patroclus was 'the fastest on his feet'. The *Iliad* also contains a description of a dramatic running race, which demonstrates how comfortable the Greeks were with physical competitiveness. After Patroclus' death, Achilles held funeral games to celebrate the dead soldier's memory and lift morale. In a contest resembling the pentathlon, Odysseus sprinted against fellow soldiers Ajax and Antilochus. Odysseus, known for his lies and tricks, was given extra speed by the goddess Athena, who also tripped Ajax, his chief rival. Ajax fell into a pile of fresh cow dung. Did the spectators condemn the foul play? 'They all roared with laughter at his expense,' wrote Homer. Odysseus was then given the prize by Achilles: a silver bowl, said by Achilles to be the best in all Greece.

This pagan braggadocio, however off-putting, is instructive. It reveals the source of pleasure: not just victory or fairness, but the basic fact of dogged exertion, displayed bodily. What mattered to the Homeric heroes were displays of physical excellence. Even if the sprinters had a divine coach slipping them supernatural steroids mid-race, the victors were celebrated. Why? Because they gave the onlookers pleasure. And the victors, in this, felt their own pride enhanced. As Hume noted, part of our pleasure in ourselves is gained in sympathy with others: we feel *their* pleasure in our success, alongside our own. This, in turn, firms up the idea we have of our own character: something more vivid, lively, intense. No doubt Odysseus smiled guilelessly as the Greeks cheered his prize, and heckled his crap-covered rival; it all increased his impression of himself.

Competition can hone this pleasure – not by giving us someone to beat, but by offering us a comparison: our self against others'. In this, exercise provides the physical proof of someone else's striving, and goads us to match or surpass it. The goal is not simply to win, but to impress upon the world the stamp of our own existence; to walk away with a heightened feeling of our own enterprise, as Odysseus did in his race with Ajax.

So exercise is not merely a way to tone muscles or increase the heart's efficiency – although it does both. It also offers a firmer idea of oneself: of the 'self' associated with bodily effort. We cannot see ourselves, this 'I' we imagine at our core. It is, as Hume noted, something of an illusion. But we can infer it with more solidity, as we watch ourselves step, pedal or lift – as we see the flesh hardening and stretching beyond its limits. Put simply, pride is the joy we feel at a more intense existential impression: a more vibrant, finely drawn self-portrait.

The Soldier's Equipment

But what *kind* of self? The stories of the *Iliad* and *Odyssey* suggest one obvious but exclusive answer: the soldier.

The Greeks were a warlike civilization, and running was obviously worthwhile because it made for fitter warriors. The *hoplitodromos* competitors sprinted in helmets and greaves, carrying shields, because that that is how they ran on the battlefield. Plato, in his dialogue *Laws*, sketched an ideal city in which citizens competed in full armour for prizes. He wanted soldiers, not professional sportsmen, striving for spectacle. 'Body agility – quickness of hand as well as of foot – is a first-rate point in the soldier's equipment,' he wrote. 'Fleetness of foot has its use in flight and pursuit.'

Obviously the same point can be made for lifting weights, athletics, gymnastics, and so on: they make us tougher, so our pride is basically martial.

But I am not a soldier – not even a policeman or bouncer. Neither are most of today's sprinters, doing laps in public parks, without the threat of rampaging Persians. Runner Cathy Freeman lives in a quiet Melbourne suburb and 'shuffles', she says, three times a week – hardly the Peloponnesian War. Power-lifter Clint Greagen might be built like the proverbial outhouse, but his days are spent folding linen (between reps) and preparing dinner.

Put simply, there is more to pride than this stereotypically masculine ideal of battlefield or back-alley toughness. The Greeks suggest a more profound, and also more democratic, idea: pride can suggest a more *responsible* character.

Try running this in 9.63 seconds, Usain; Greeks sprint in armour.

Racing Feet and Striving Hands

In the *Iliad*, the soldiers did not simply sprint for battle. They also ran
to commemorate Patroclus' memory. He was a famed sprinter, and the
running races recalled his physical and moral virtues. As the crowds
cheered 'shining long-enduring Odysseus', they recalled Patroclus.
This was more than a sporting eulogy for the slain. It was a reminder
for the living: glory in your muscles and lungs while you can.

Likewise in Homer's *Odyssey*. Odysseus was, by this stage, middle-
aged, weary and grumpy. Shipwrecked on Phaeacia, he was feasted
by the king, but privately wept for his wife, son and island, Ithaca.
To cheer him up, King Alcinous did exactly what Achilles did after
Patroclus' death: he held games. To taunt Odysseus into the contest,
Prince Laodamas said: 'What glory attends a man, while he's alive, than
what he wins with his racing feet and striving hands?' The wording
makes it clear: tough luck, mate, but there is no point moping. Get off
your bum and enjoy your muscles while you have them.

Odysseus replied angrily, but was soon sucked into competition.
He won the discus in a single throw, and then insulted the youths:

> Not match *that*, you young pups, and straightaway
> I'll hurl another just as far, I swear, or even further!
> All the rest of you, anyone with spine and spirit,
> Step right up and try me – you've incensed me so –
>
> at boxing, wrestling, racing; nothing daunts me.

Note the combination of intense pride and regained confidence.
Like all of the Greek heroes, Odysseus is proud of his muscularity

and speed. The youths goad him into competition, and this works: he loses his sullen tears, and walks proudly again. Put in Hume's language, by regaining pleasure in his body, Odysseus enhances his idea of himself. This is because the relations of ideas and passions move both ways. Joy can bring with it an existential responsibility: this is *my* body, my life, and I will not be beaten by age or acrimony.

Odysseus' pride is echoed in the words of Pindar, a fifth-century BC Greek poet. No stranger to running races or pride, Pindar was paid by games victors to celebrate their conquests. In 498 BC, he wrote a song for Hippokleas, winner of the double sprint in the Pythian games. 'The gods may feel no sorrow, but a man should be accounted happy and worthy of song,' he said of Hippokleas, 'if boldness and power have gained him the greatest prize for the might of hand and foot.'

This emphasis on mortality highlights our human responsibility. For the Greeks, the gods had eternity to enjoy caprice and play. They did not get ill or old. We humans have a short span of life, and an even shorter span of prime fitness. 'If a man attains his wish let him cling to it and not let it go for something far off,' Pindar wrote for Hippokleas the sprinter. 'There is no telling what will be a year from now.' Enjoy your triumph, says Pindar, because life is brief and brutal. He cautions competitors against *hubris*: transgressing the sacred laws of men and gods. He damns avarice and cruelty. But for Pindar, physical pride is not only pleasurable, but also virtuous. It is rightful pleasure in activity instead of passivity – in stubborn exertion, which makes the most of precarious flesh.

Question: Remind yourself of life's fragility and shortness before exercise. Does it change your performance, or how you feel about it?

Be the Rock

This message from the Greeks is simple but profound, and transcends their civilization. There is, as Hume argued with devastating precision, no happy afterlife, no cosmic plan for the redemption of immortal souls. We *are* bodies, and we will suffer and die – all of us, without exception. In this, the pagan outlook is surprisingly modern. But this grim disclosure can also be a source of pleasure. It is precisely because intense muscular effort is so fragile and ephemeral that it is bliss. When Odysseus met him in the Underworld, Achilles famously said he would prefer to be a servant to a poor man than a dead king of kings. To live, however lowly and briefly, is a chance to strive.

So pride in exercise is more than a firmer idea of ourselves, of the 'I' we imagine we are. It is also a sense of the worth of this achievement: that, with limited days and vitality, we still bother to hone ourselves by striving physically. Given all the possible ways to sit idle, and to justify this, we have dedicated ourselves to some act of uncomfortable toil.

This is why, as Pindar suggested and Hume argued, pride is also a kind of virtue. In the pride of sprinting, power-lifting or pedalling, we rightly celebrate ourselves for our committed exertion; for the willingness to move as hard and fast as we possibly can, instead of watching others do so on television. We are, in short, exerting *ourselves* when we might equally not.

This takes not only fitness, but also a keen sense of responsibility: recognition that we might die tomorrow having never touched the edges of our own abilities. This is less about 'seizing the day', and other positive-thinking slogans, and more about more firmly grasping ourselves: as fragile, precarious things, with a small portion of vitality. We cannot wait for God or gods to give us our souls – the self is something we must continually, often consciously, create. In this, exercise is a recollection of the burden of existence, which gives us pleasure as we lift it.

The French philosopher Albert Camus, famous for his love of soccer, once argued that Sisyphus, rolling the boulder up the hill for eternity, was happy. It was *his* rock – that is, his duty, his task, and no one else's. The pride of exercise offers this same strained happiness, only *we* are the rock.

3. Sacrifice

As a teenager, tennis allowed me to make sacrifices: nothing grand, but certainly losses of selfishness and comfort. I gave up my egotism and my Saturdays, or I forfeited the game.

Games like tennis, football and almost all competitive exercises have rules and rituals that set them apart from normal life. They can provide a second universe, which asks for toil and pain, but gives us a more simple existence in return – an existence we can walk away from when it becomes too much.

'Mine'

I am fourteen, and wearing my regular Saturday tennis uniform: black tracksuit bottoms, black hoodie and black Los Angeles Raiders baseball cap.

In my hands is a new graphite racquet, handle freshly wrapped in bright red tape. I twirl it left and right, slowly, as I listen to Matt bouncing the ball behind me, to my right.

Like me, Matt is a shorter-than-average, bad-tempered player, not given to pleasantries. Unlike me, Matt is also a talented sprinter and footballer. We are not mates. I refuse to be impressed by his reputed physical gifts, obvious popularity or cute girlfriend, and he (quite rightly) believes I am an awkward nerd with a big mouth.

But as I stand at the net, staring down the lanky, freckled redhead awaiting Matt's serve, none of this bothers me. We are not in the locker rooms, pushing one another roughly to get to bags and pull-overs. We are not in English class, trading in snark. Matt and I are on the tennis court, and the usual rules do not apply.

He fires one of his cannonball serves over the net. It just misses my right ear, then bounces just inside the far left quarter. Ace.

40–30. Set point.

Matt serves again, the ball bouncing about three inches past the left baseline: a fault. His second serve is generic, and the redhead sends it back to me fast and hard from the baseline. I volley, the ball angling behind the redhead's partner, a heavy boy in fluores-cent orange shorts and a whiter-than-white Lacoste polo shirt. The redhead leaps to his right, lobbing the ball above me. Perfectly above me, in fact: just right for a smash.

Now is the moment of glory. I am Thor, stringed hammer in my hands. I will destroy Master Lacoste, smashing the ball down over the net. He and the redhead can see it in my eyes. And . . .

Matt calls out 'mine'.

Oh.

I want to say 'no', but I trust him. This is a risk, because I am perfectly placed to pummel this ball. And our opponents are readying themselves for a hard and fast return. Having lost time running up from the baseline, will Matt be at the right angle to smack the ball hard?

No. And he does not try. He volleys gently over the net, tapping under the ball with his left forehand. A drop shot. Lacoste and the redhead sprint from behind the baseline to catch the ball. Almost.

But Matt's backspin is just right. The ball drops onto the clay and bounces back toward the net, just out of reach.

Victory.

It is a strange but familiar Saturday-morning ritual. I have given up on my on-court grandeur, putting it in the hands of a teammate – and one I am not friendly with. I have put my epic ears at risk for the sake of a fast serve. And I am quietly happy about it all.

I have enjoyed this contentment when playing soccer: limping off the field with bruises from studded boots in my shin while the striker kicks a goal. In Australian-rules football, too: getting knocked over while marking (catching) the ball, then quickly hand-passing it to one of my faster teammates (probably Matt).

This is the odd joy that comes from sacrifice: giving up something of my own – often glory or comfort – for the sake of another. But why do I feel this way?

Question: What do you give up when you exercise? Does it always feel like an unpleasant deprivation?

Serving a 'Certain Being'

To understand the satisfaction of sacrifice, it helps to understand what we are sacrificing *for*.

The most basic fact of playing a sport is that we are 'playing'. This is partly the mindset of 'flow', which we will encounter later. But there is another aspect to play: pretending. There are a handful of words in English – sport, game, play – which all mean roughly the same thing, and which have a double meaning: competitive exercises, but also jokes or fun. 'Do I look to be in a gaming mood?' asks Thor of Loki, in superhero film *The Avengers*. The point: the god of thunder is not kidding around. Something 'sportive' is light-hearted. Game animals are animals hunted for amusement. A play is a work of theatre: of pretending, not real life.

Yet sport is not a superficial mock-up; not something insubstantial or inconsequential. Sports are an arena of genuine striving, pain and loss. Witness one of the most legendary matches of Australian-rules football, a sport known for its aggressive physicality. In the 1989 grand final, Hawthorn player Robert DiPierdomenico was running backwards to mark the ball when he was knocked from behind by Geelong star Gary Ablett. DiPierdomenico continued to play for the rest of the game, despite his pain. After the final siren, he collapsed. Rushed to casualty, DiPierdomenico ended up in intensive care: the power of Ablett's bump had broken several of DiPierdomenico's ribs, and punctured his lung. 'I had eight days in hospital to think about what might have happened,' he said. 'To tell you the truth, it scared me.'

Obviously DiPierdomenico was a professional footballer, and a particularly robust one at that. But this *kind* of sacrifice is well known in amateur sports and exercise: from the countless schoolkids getting kicked, tackled and thwacked with hockey sticks every weekend, to the ultramarathon runners getting sunburnt in Death Valley, to the swimmers up at four in the morning to do laps. Less painfully, there was teenaged me, giving up my tennis apotheosis (and relaxed weekend). All kinds of play, and all kinds of sacrifice.

In short: sport and competitive exercise are make-believe pursuits that *matter*. They are simultaneously trivial and profoundly important.

This is because they are a second world, of sorts. J. R. R. Tolkien, the author of *Lord of the Rings* and *The Hobbit*, was not much of a cricket fan. But he recognized make-believe when he saw it. In a little essay entitled 'On Fairy-Stories', Tolkien wrote about what he called 'enchantment': the creation of another world, which exists alongside our everyday reality. Authors like Tolkien are creators of this kind: he calls them 'sub-creators'. The author, says Tolkien, 'makes a Secondary World which your mind can enter. Inside it, what he relates is "true": it accords with the laws of that world.' When inside one of these worlds, we are not 'suspending disbelief', as if this were a trick of the mind. Instead, we are wholly committing to the world's rules. Only those with no commitment to the creation must suspend disbelief. And Tolkien saw this happening in sport alongside literary fantasy. 'A real enthusiast for cricket is in the enchanted state: Secondary Belief,' he wrote. 'I, when I watch a match, am on the lower level. I can achieve . . . willing suspension of disbelief.'

Importantly, one of the hallmarks of the secondary world of sport is that it is *not* the primary one. But this does not mean that play is somehow fake. Sociologist Pierre Bourdieu points out that ordinary business, schooling and family are also games of sorts – forms of what Tolkien calls 'enchantment'. They have rules, winners and losers, and rewards. The laws of society, which divide us into classes, genders, neighbourhoods, professions, are just as artificial as those that say a tennis ball outside a white line means defeat. But we often grow up believing they are unquestioningly, unavoidably real. And we invest in them: part of our love of life, and of ourselves, is tied up with our income, professional kudos or parental wizardry. Bourdieu calls this *illusio*: the stakes of the game of life, and our commitment to these stakes. 'One does not

The state of
enchantment,
c. 1944.

embark on the game by a conscious act, one is born into the game, with the game,' Bourdieu writes, 'and the relation of . . . *illusio*, investment, is made more total and unconditional by the fact that it is unaware of what it is.' In other words, to devote oneself to the secondary world of tennis or marathon races is not to give up on reality for a false show. It is to choose, however briefly, one game over another.

Both games ask for sacrifices of comfort, selfishness and fantasy. Desk jobs can wither muscles and squander hours with loved ones; can demand missed sleep and constant anxiety. And the sacrifices of exercise – from pinched nerves, to miserably cold weekend practice sessions, to regular reminders of inadequacy or incompetence – are obvious even to spectators. To commit, as a human being, to *anything* is to renounce some quantum of pleasure – a measure that is enlarged by every increase in dedication. Every game exacts a cost.

But the sacrifices of exercise are often more satisfying, because its rules are clearer and simpler than those of workaday existence. Society has laws and competition, but these are often subtle or complicated. For all our intuitive knowledge of class and status, suggested by accent, clothes and musical tastes – what Bourdieu calls a 'feel for the game' – we can still find relationships uncertain and unnerving. For example, high school was, for me, a continual (failed) endeavour to comprehend. How to relate to others – honesty versus tactful lies, sexual innuendo versus false purity, physical aggression versus symbolic manipulation – was puzzling. Life was (and continues to be) a condition of ambiguity.

But on the tennis court none of this mattered. I knew that 40 followed 30, and that a left foot over the line when serving was a foot fault. In soccer, there was no question of what subjects to pick, and what profession I was to take up: my job was to stop strikers from the other team kicking the ball past me. Even the most extreme physical endeavours can be simpler than 'real life'. 'As daunting as it would be to run for twenty to thirty hours straight,' wrote Dean Karnazes in *Ultramarathon Man*, 'at least I knew what was expected of me. There would be a starting line, and 100 miles from that a finish line. All I needed to do was run from here to there.'

Jean-Paul Sartre, in *Being and Nothingness*, noted how painful human existence can be: how we are always a question for ourselves. Because we are free, we are fundamentally ambiguous. We cannot shake liberty. There is never a moment, in life, when we can say: now I am perfect (just 'being', in Sartre's words). But sport and exercise give us a chance to be something *specific* for a short time; to grasp and possess ourselves like a thing; to say, 'I am *this* now'. 'The first principle of play is man himself,' writes Sartre. 'His goal, which he aims at through sports . . . or games, is to attain himself as a certain being'.

This 'certain being' is partly why we have uniforms, formal etiquette and rituals in sport: tennis whites (or blacks, in my case), handshakes after the match, Wimbledon champion Serena Williams bouncing the ball five times before a first serve and twice before the second. These practices help to develop the mindset of the game – like religious vestments and incense, they encourage the transition from one world to the next. They are like existential props, which allow us to block out parts of the world and ourselves that conflict with the game, and our ability to play it well.

The game can also afford a straightforward role to complement the rules. I become a server or receiver, a striker or goalie or full back – the dilemmas of identity evaporate.

This is why cheating can be so loathsome: not simply because it allows victory without effort, but because it punctures the balloon of play. If we are all following the rules, the state of enchantment continues. But the moment another competitor cheats, the artifice is revealed, and we are wrenched from our secondary world. The problem is not that this world is pretend – it is no more pretend than the market, or education rankings. The problem is that it undermines freedom, by destroying our choice to commit to this world, and the 'specific being' it affords. Cheating cracks our blissful clarity.

When it works, exercise can be a reprieve from confusion – from the anxiety that comes with not knowing one's place in the world. It involves sacrifice, as does schooling, marriage and work. But sport allows us to say, with far more confidence, whether we have won or lost, and played the game well. The blisters, muscle aches and dawn wake-up calls are the price paid for a temporarily simpler existence.

Confession: I rarely played tennis well – my coach called me a 'fine social player'. But it was no less liberating for this.

A World We Can Give Up

The 'temporarily' is vital. Competitive exercise is also a world we can give up. 'Society,' writes Bourdieu in his book *Pascalian Meditations*, 'is God.' Bourdieu's point is not that the primary world is supernatural or interested in damnation or grace. His point is that we cannot ever escape from society. We are social animals, and our early lives are spent leaning what it is to be human: we are in *this* family, of

Sharing the secondary world.

this gender, *this* ethnicity, and we commit to these industries or voca-
tions, or to the varieties of unemployment. These are not just ideas.
Our bodies are shown how to walk (swagger or hunch, swinging or
hulking arms), eat (fork up or down, dessert or soup spoon), dress
(bespoke or off-the-shelf, uniform or casual, skin exposed or covered),
and so on. And we are also taught to *care* about these things: this is
the *illusio*. We are, to a greater or lesser extent, imprisoned in society,
and devoted to our jail.

Bourdieu notes that this confinement is something of a compro-
mise. As young children, we have to give up on our narcissism:
we cannot simply love ourselves, straightforwardly, as infants do.
Instead, we invest our desire in our parents, and then in the institutions that they represent: schools, jobs, and so on. The more we
succeed at becoming the kinds of humans society values – good children, good students, good workers – the more we are recognized by
society. We are given awards, prizes, raises, dinner parties, and so on.
What Bourdieu calls, in *Pascalian Meditations*, 'the search for recognition', is nothing other than a slow rediscovery and reclaiming of
what we lost as children: love of self. We cannot do it directly, so we
do it indirectly: through the approval and applause of others.

Because we invest so much in the primary world – *the* world, in
other words – the secondary world of exercise and sport is a welcome
break. We still commit to it heartily. But it does not have the same
power over us. The *illusio* is more freely given: it is an investment
of choice, not birth, upbringing and schooling. This is why Sartre
emphasizes freedom in sport, describing it as 'creative like art'. We
sacrifice our comfort and glory, but on our *own* terms. The world is
transformed into a backdrop for our emancipated striving. In tennis,

I play as hard and fast as I can, and I enjoy it when I win; enjoy the handshake of my doubles partner, after he takes his winning shot. But, win or lose, it matters as much as I *let* it matter.

Obviously, exercise can also become burdensome, particularly for professionals for whom a few hundredths of a second can mean the difference between success and failure, lucrative sponsorship and poor obscurity. The secondary world shrinks, so that release is enjoyed briefly – if at all. Often the primary and secondary worlds merge. Sport is no longer an escape from the usual pressures: income, status, social friction. But for us amateurs, sporting competition can be a break from the games of ordinary life. We are always playing in some way, but the secondary world of sport or exercise provides the love without the imprisonment. It asks for sacrifices of blood and ego, but not of liberty.

4. Beauty

Weights training: picking up and pushing heavy things, over and over again. Then gazing: at ourselves, and others – often in wall-to-ceiling mirrors. For many today, the quest for fitness goes hand-in-hand with a desire for beauty.

This is not a modern invention. From the ancient Greeks, to Renaissance sculptors, to Arnold Schwarzenegger, the muscular body has offered aesthetic joy: the pleasure of bringing new proportions and harmonies into the world. We can enjoy this beauty for its own sake, without giving in to narcissism.

Mirrors

The late 1990s. I am an Honours student, visiting my friend Mike in the city. Dressed in camel cords, a stiff, oversized white shirt and second-hand tweed jacket (because I am an Honours student, you see), I lope into the gym where Mike works part-time.

Mike is in a thin branded tank-top, doing biceps curls. I stand to his left. Facing the mirrored wall, we watch his arm muscles swell. I count each repetition aloud, in a falsely authoritative voice, saying things like, 'C'mon, one more, one more.' Mike lets the curl bar fall onto the rack and, breathing out heavily, strikes a pose: arms curled up, biceps high and round, abdominals sucked in and down, like neatly fitted puzzle pieces.

A tanned twenty-something with cornrow braids and a 'V' torso stops, looks at Mike's reflection and nods with a smile. Pointing at Mike's arms with a connoisseur's squinted eyes, she stage whispers: 'Look at that double bicep vein. You're a freak.'

Mike laughs knowingly and studies his arms some more. 'My biceps,' he says, pointing calmly at the balls of muscle, like Kenneth Clark in his *Civilisation* series, judging the Apollo Belvedere. 'They're too small for my shoulders. Like tennis balls next to cannonballs.'

Still, Mike is generally pleased by his reflection – as are most of the gym members, gazing at his shiny muscles over stacked bar-bells, between sips of Musashi protein drink. Others look at themselves instead: in the floor-to-ceiling mirrors, or in shop and car windows. The hulks, models and Olympians are putting on a show: for others, but also for themselves.

In this, they are only doing publicly what many do in private. The fitness industry today is partly devoted to buffed beauty: low body fat and visible muscles in 'balanced' proportions. Since the 1970s, this bodybuilding ideal has become mainstream: the hallmark of athletes, actors and celebrities, and many ordinary folk on the bench press, or rowing machine.

If we fall short of superstar abdominals, the slow development of muscularity and lower fat is still something we savour: in gymnasium and bathroom mirrors, shop windows, and the looks of strangers. It is why Olympian Jessica Ennis's abdominals are more popular than the sport of hurdling will ever be; why footballer David Beckham's stomach features in underwear advertisements, not his right foot.

However much we care for health, most of us who exercise enjoy the beauty it affords. But why? What is pleasurable about harder muscles on a leaner body?

Fitness

Partly because muscles are useful. Hume, as we saw, tied beauty to pleasure, and pleasure to value. To enjoy the look of hard biceps is to recognize their worth: as means to some end.

This definition of beauty can be summed up with a modern motto: 'form follows function'. But it was actually a common idea in ancient Greece, the historical home of muscled youths and the statues that immortalized them. 'All that is beautiful,' says Socrates in Plato's *Gorgias*, 'whether in body, colour, form, sound, or activity, would . . . be classed as such by reference to some purpose.' To fulfil this purpose, a certain harmony is necessary: parts fitting together perfectly to make a whole. So the human body is beautiful when its proportions suggest strength, speed, skill.

His student Aristotle, in his *Politics*, made the same argument, noting that handsome and righteous men were above average because of 'the assembly and unification of features otherwise dispersed.' We enjoy not just the biceps and triceps, but the jutting arcs of a whole arm, which balances the shoulders, chest and waist. Aristotle also added an extra point: while proportion is the standard of beauty, this standard changes with age and profession. A middle-aged man, built for war, he said in *Rhetoric*, is 'pleasant and formidable', whereas a youth's beauty implies 'the possession of a body built for exertion, whether speed or power.' (Slaves did slave work, and had slaves' bodies.) What the springy athlete and knotted old soldier have in common is a useful body: one in which the muscles are harmonized by some overall pursuit.

Importantly, ancient Greek males have no monopoly on this. Author and champion boxer Mischa Merz enjoyed the power of her muscles, gained while training to fight. 'I noticed my shoulders and arms were beginning to look "cut",' she writes in *Bruising*. 'Nice plaited details . . . came out, particularly when I skipped.' Merz later won a coveted Golden Gloves belt in New York.

This is why we still call it 'fitness': because it is fit *for* something. In this sense, to savour the beauty that arises with exercise is to respond to the promise of accomplishment. Whether or not we actually achieve anything is neither here nor there. The point is that the increasing visibility of muscles suggests increasing potency: the circle of our influence has widened. This, in turn, can be uplifting or comforting: the knowledge that, should we be challenged or threatened, we have more resources at our disposal. Muscularity is an antidote to a more general human condition: insecurity and uncertainty.

Question: What are your muscles for? How does your physique reflect your occupation or lifestyle?

Geometry Buff

But do we always enjoy fitness for its usefulness? Often not. 'The groups of muscles that have become virtually unnecessary in modern life,' wrote Japanese novelist and bodybuilder Yukio Mishima in *Sun and Steel*, 'are obviously pointless from a practical point of view, and bulging muscles are as unnecessary as a classical education is to the majority of practical men.'

In fact, massive muscularity does not even guarantee practical strength (and certainly not health). Oxford graduate and bodybuilder Sam Fussell, in his book *Muscle*, makes the point viscerally. 'I couldn't run twenty yards without pulling up and gasping for air. My ass cheeks ached from innumerable steroid injections,' he wrote, 'my stomach whined for sustenance . . . my face was drawn and haggard, my eyes the haunted sockets of a ghoul.'

So muscles are not always the means to some straightforward end. Instead, we often savour the look of a more toned body *for* its look – that is, for its own sake.

To understand this, it is helpful to turn back to the Greeks. Plato, for example, thought that the muscular proportion of an athletic boy was actually *more* important than his fitness for sport or battle. It actually suggested a proportionate soul, in which emotion, reason and will were properly balanced.

This was partly because of the virtues required to be a successful athlete, like courage, perseverance and temperance. But it was also because the soul itself was, at its best, in a kind of harmony. And beyond the soul was the ultimate reality, which mathematics, argued Plato, helped us to comprehend.

Aristotle was not quite so idealistic, but he had the same interest in ideal harmony. 'The greatest species of beauty are order, proportion, and limit,' he wrote in his *Metaphysics*, 'which are above all the objects of mathematical research.'

So physical beauty, for both thinkers, was a precise fitting-together of parts and wholes: a unity of measure. And this unity was basically mathematical. Both philosophers also believed that beauty was not necessarily *enjoyed* with use in mind. For all its visceral allure, the beautiful body had an ideal value.

This ideal remains today. It is one of the most characteristic legacies of the Greek world: an ideal of harmony, balance, proportion. In this classical vision, muscles are an intimation of higher things: men and women displaying 'natural' beauty.

Here, 'nature' is code for 'geometric'. It is no coincidence that one of the great ancient Greek sculptors, Polyclitus, claimed to have an ideal ratio for his statues of athletes. The sculptor gave his famous *Doryphoros* ('Spear-Bearer') a relaxed pose, but behind the calm was calculation.

Over two millennia after Polyclitus, modern bodybuilders and other weightlifters still speak in the geometric language of classical sculpture. 'The ideal of bodybuilding is visual perfection, like an ancient Greek statue come to life. You sculpt your body the way an artist chisels stone,' wrote seven-times Mr Olympia Arnold Schwarzenegger. 'The judges in the top competitions scrutinize every detail: muscle size, definition, proportion, and symmetry.' Australian power-lifter and bodybuilder Bev Francis tried to show judges that there was nothing 'masculine' about her own classical body. 'I want to show them that a woman can develop muscle and still look like a woman and look strong,' she said in the documentary *Pumping Iron II*, 'and look like a statue, like a Greek god.'

The point is not that athletes must also be geometers. The point is that muscular bodies can suggest more than power for punching or

A handsome equation: the *Doryphoros* of Polyclitus.

courting. Someone lifting the curl bar or doing push-ups is revealing a classical archetype. Hence all the posing and preening. It is not simply egotism and vanity: the increasingly visible muscles often point beyond the flesh, to some apprehension of higher laws – what Mishima called 'a universal aspect'.

I Am Not a Pineapple

But is there *really* a universal form of human muscular beauty? No. Since Polyclitus, various sculptors, painters, architects, scientists and conspiracy theorists have spoken of magical mathematical ratios and sequences.

One of the most famous proportions is the 'Golden Ratio' (1.618), known as *phi* (Φ), after Phidias the Greek artist. The Golden Ratio appears in plants, including leaves and fruit. The sharp whorls on pineapples, for example, follow pairs of numbers – called the Fibonacci series – that converge on *phi*. According to psychologist Vladimir Konečni, the Golden Ratio also turns up in some beautiful faces and figures in art, and in modern geometric works by artists like Mondrian. In other words, the Golden Ratio seems like a universal rule of beauty: something common to plants, animals and the buffed bodies of human animals. One *Men's Health* feature wrote breathlessly that the Golden Ratio can be found in the Parthenon, Leonardo's Vitruvian Man and Michelangelo's *David*, and the ultimate male body: 'chicks dig a physique that measures up to the golden ratio.'

But we are not pineapples. It pays to be careful with mystical numerical secrets. While Konečni's studies are carefully controlled, many of these popular 'discoveries' of *phi* are vague approximations. Mathematician George Markowsky has pointed out many Golden Ratio falsehoods: there is no evidence that it is the basis of the Parthenon, the Egyptian pyramids, Leonardo's drawings, or Polyclitus' 'Spear-Bearer'. (Well, *half* of the statue, says Markowsky, has rough *phi* proportions.) The chest-to-waist ratio of the Edwardian era's 'perfect man', Eugen Sandow, was 1.655. (If Sandow's publicity can be believed.)

And even if *phi* is found in chest-to-waist or head–navel–knee ratios, it does not necessarily move or excite us. In one of Konečni's studies, artists actually copied artworks more faithfully when *phi* was involved – as if the ratio commanded a certain respect. But ordinary psychology students, with no artistic training, were often more interested in balance than in *phi*. We are not *all* struck dumb by a sports star's abdominals or actor's pectorals, however geometrically 'perfect' – education, mood and circumstances change our enjoyment.

Put simply, beauty is not as universal as the classical ideal suggests. It has sweet spots, but they are vague and variable – certainly not written into the fabric of the cosmos. It is important to own up to our own conceit: with exercise (and often diet), we are crafting our *own* ideal. But how does this personal ideal work?

Confession: My chest-to-waist ratio is 1.25.

An Experience of Beauty

The philosopher John Dewey argued that our enjoyment of beauty is never purely intellectual or purely spiritual. Instead, it involves the whole human being, including our basic instincts. And one of these instincts is for unity.

For Dewey, we are not cut off from the world: not thinking atoms, discrete and divided. We are physical creatures within environments, trying to get by. We act upon the world, it acts upon us – there is an interplay that never lets up, even when we are asleep. 'The career and destiny of a living being,' wrote Dewey in his *Art as Experience*, 'are bound up with its interchanges with its environment, not externally but in the most intimate way.' Dewey calls this 'experience'.

Experience never ends, of course – this is what it means to be alive. But we can find a brief equilibrium when we no longer strain or suffer. Often these moments are not passive, argues Dewey, but active. We marshal our energies, and those of the environment, to make new order out of disorder, new rhythms in time and space. 'In this interaction, human energy gathers, is released, dammed up, frustrated and victorious,' wrote Dewey. 'There are rhythms of want and fulfilment, pulses of doing and being withheld from doing.'

In this way, we transform experience into what Dewey called *an* experience. An experience is a unity: a part of life that has some form of its own. It has a beginning, middle and end; a radius and circumference; or a trunk, torso and head. It catches the eye with beauty, but its gift is more primal than prettiness or charm: a brief reprieve from the flux and tangle of life. And this is exactly what happens when we build muscle.

First, we are involved in Dewey's 'interchange' with the environment, which has rhythms: twirling the caps on bar-bells; sliding steel plates on and off; ten or fifteen repetitions (breathing in to rest, breathing out to strain); feeling strength or breath ebb and flow before the final clang of bar on hooks or thud of kettle-bell on concrete. Power-lifter Clint Greagen wrote that 'rhythm can come during a set from setting up, drawing in breath and performing each repetition.' Note the specific rituals:

> Wrist wraps go on as I eye off the weight and remind myself
> of form. I sit on the bench, hunched a little, a deep breath. I
> lie back on to the bench with my head forward of the bar and
> map out my grip by placing my little fingers on the rings.

Like the cadence of a jog, return-and-volley of tennis, or punch-block-kick of a karate form, this rhythm is satisfying in itself. Rhythm also marks each day and week, as we follow exercise routines.

Second, when working out we are actually introducing *new* order: burning calories and then fat, and tearing muscles to help them grow bigger and stronger. There is no longer a smooth softness in the upper arm: the biceps become higher and more rounded, and the triceps divide from the deltoid in the shoulder; veins, previously covered by fat, now outline the muscles. This is what the bodybuilding word 'defined' really means: in refining muscles, we are helping to define our own physical form. Biceps curls, kettle-bell swings and push-ups are a species of bodily art: developing *an* experience from the experience of our own skin. Likewise for any exercise that strips away fat, or changes the architecture of our physique.

This *seems* purely ideal, because it involves common human physiology – it looks 'natural', as Mishima believed. And the feelings of an aesthetic experience – harmony and completeness, for example – can suggest a stillness and wholeness at odds with messy, piecemeal life.

But biology and taste are too varied for there to be one simple ideal. There is no one human archetype – there are only types, and they are as artificial as they are natural. 'The symmetry you got, Louis,' said Matty Ferrigno to his son, Mr Olympia competitor Lou Ferrigno, in the film *Pumping Iron* 'You know, you look like something Michelangelo cut out.' But, no: Ferrigno was something *Ferrigno* cut out – something new.

Question: Look at your nude body in a mirror. Note the different patterns of muscle, skin and bone. Experiment with different poses, lighting, angles. What parts are beautiful? Why?

Looking for 'Me' in all the Wrong Places

Is all this muscular mirror-gazing just narcissism? Sometimes, yes. But narcissism is not simply a love of oneself: a vain drooling over one's own oily reflection. In fact, narcissists have what is now known in pop psychology as 'poor self-esteem'. Symptoms of narcissism include grandiosity, fantasies of power and dominance, feelings of emptiness, low empathy for others, exploitativeness. Narcissists do not have the Doryphoros' serenity: they crave applause, fear and worship because they cannot provide their *own* praise and respect.

If this reads like a description of Arnold Schwarzenegger in the documentary *Pumping Iron*, as he taunts Lou Ferrigno and swaggers around every room, it is no coincidence. Several studies report that bodybuilders score highly on narcissism tests. While steroid users are often more aggressive, cruel and concerned with their own

Cutting myself out – with sixteen kilograms of iron.

supremacy, bodybuilding as a whole can often be what psychologist Gidi Rubinstein calls an 'overcompensation for inferiority feelings'. To be, is to be *seen* to be.

Obviously most of us are not bodybuilders. We will not have these Olympians' mania for size and striations. The hyper-masculine 'grandiosity and excess' discovered by Alan Klein in his book *Little Big Men* is nothing to most suburban gym-bunnies or garage-sweaters, heaving bar-bells and stretching themselves in 'the plank'.

Still, as we eye up our deltoids and abdominals in the mirror, it is important to remember that our pleasure is literally superficial: on the surface of ourselves. As an aesthetic experience, it does not necessarily make us smarter, healthier, a better lover or fighter. It is no licence to dominate or exploit. And it does not make us any more of a 'man' or 'woman'. It is simply a visual achievement: *an* experience of muscles and skin. As the poet and philosopher Friedrich Schiller noted in his *On the Aesthetic Education of Man in a Series of Letters*, there is nothing wrong with semblance: spectacle, show, exhibition. The important thing is not to confuse it with reality.

In this light, the beauty of fitness involves two kinds of discipline. The first is obvious: the strain behind the striations. The second is more subtle, but equally vital: the ability to savour bodily charm without giving in to its intimations of grandeur, to seek aesthetic pleasure without vanity. This might mean posters of Polyclitus or Michelangelo sculptures on the wall, instead of the latest Mr Olympia; might mean an interest in pencils and clay rather than protein bars and ever-heavier lifting. The point is to train the eye to see muscles as aesthetic achievements, not existential props.

Tip: Visit an art museum and take a muscular tour of the ages. Compare your physique to those in classical, medieval and modern artworks. How did the Greeks of the fourth-century BC depict the body, next to Pieter Brueghel or the Italian Futurists?

5. Humility

Rock climbing and mountaineering suggest a certain madness or machismo: doomed explorers freezing on mountain-tops, or Sylvester Stallone exploding his way across the Dolomites.

But climbing can encourage humility: not wallflower meekness, but an awareness of our own flaws and limitations. Humility also nudges us to pay attention: to the demands of the exercise, and how we can meet them. This careful consciousness is a reward in itself: the 'flow' of a body and mind, merging with the exercise.

High Humility

I am up against the wall – literally. The wall is plywood, covered in cement render, and painted to look like rock. Somewhere between a gym and an 'alien planet' set from *Star Trek*, this is the Hard Rock climbing centre.

My fingers, locked into small plastic holds, are stiff and white. My left forearm feels oddly swollen: like the skin cannot contain the muscles and blood.

With my stronger right hand, I reach above my head to the next hold, which looks like an oversized purple ear. But my left arm is starting to cramp. I swap hands, letting my left rest briefly as I reach up. No. The next hold (more like a miniature Jean Arp sculpture) is too high. Can I use my legs to push up? No. I am on tiptoes already, balancing awkwardly on an inch of plastic.

In short, I am stuck: forty feet in the air, my limbs failing with fatigue.

After a minute of clumsy swipes and whispered swearing, my left hand seizes up. Stuck in a stiff 'c' like a Lego hand, it is useless. I let go.

Back arched in a self-conscious pose of messianic defeat, arms splayed by my sides, I'm lowered by ropes to the floor. Shaking my head, I look around. Thirty feet up, to my right, a woman in a tank-top and tights is calmly chalking her fingers. No sign of my anxiety. Near the gym entrance, a lean twenty-something, his skating cap backwards, is jumping from hold to hold like gravity is just a hallucination of the heavy. Easy.

I sit on a couch for ten minutes, rotating my wrists and wriggling my fingers. When they start working, I try again – and fail again. I try an easier level: good old level fourteen. No luck. Not because the wall's higher or steeper. Not because holds have moved. But because my hands and arms are now too weak to hold my weight. I am obviously beaten: by physiology and physics.

And this is not even a real crag. No unstable ice spikes, no sharp granite, no falling snow dislodging pitons and pummelling arms. The room is air-conditioned, and has a well-stocked drinks fridge.

Humbling.

Indoor rock climbing: a losing battle against physiology and physics.

Humility by Hume

What is humility? Hume, as we saw, revealed the nature of pride: borrowed pleasure, which begins in some part of us and is lent to the whole. Humility is the same, only what's felt is pain, not pleasure. It is not just the physical discomfort, though this is part of all climbs – what Isabella Lucy Bird, in 1879, having climbed Longs Peak in Colorado, called 'painful and unwilling submission to the inevitable'. Instead, it is psychological pain: I feel humble because I perceive some ugliness in myself, and this is uncomfortable, unpleasant. *My* slight forearms and weak fingers are paralysed.

This is not a pain reserved for outdoorsy sorts on walls or mountains. Superstar gymnast Nadia Comaneci, in *Letters to a Young Gymnast*, writes of the humiliation of her first competition. 'With my first high leap, I fell off the beam. Embarrassed, I climbed back on and immediately fell off the right side . . . My ears burned with the imagined laughter of my teammates and other competitors.'

Humility is worse in public, said Hume, because I perceive – rightly or wrongly – others' judgement alongside my own, and their feelings make mine more forceful. Their victories also make my weaknesses seem more damning; in this gym of wiry, nimble monkeys, I am a fat old Labrador: heavy, clumsy, breathless.

These feelings can pass, says Hume, if what causes one's failure is accidental. For example, I might be addled with a virus, so my pitiful half-climb does not reflect my normally superhuman wall skills. (But, no: I'm fine.) I can also avoid the pain of humility by trivializing others' achievements. By seeing their successes as fleeting or just good luck, I remove the comparison with myself. I might say to myself: *all these wall-conquistadors are younger, have no children and have hours free between university classes – soon they will be frail and inept like me.* (But, no: there are middle-aged office-workers shimmying up the wall. Suck it up, Damon.)

So my Hard Rock humility is a psychological pain, worsened amongst more talented peers. When my limbs give up, they present me with an unpalatable vision of myself: feeble, uncoordinated, easily tired.

Fear's Kindly Sister

Why am I subjecting myself to this? Next to pride, this humility seems like something to avoid. As we saw, pride can nudge us to reclaim ourselves; to find, in pleasure, a new responsibility for living. Humility has a touch of Christian meekness to it; a mood of sackcloth and forelock-tugging. Yet humility, for Hume, had no religious basis. It was a straightforwardly secular response to one's own perceived ugliness. But, if not squashing the psyche to make room for God, what is the point of this discomfort?

The value of humility is greater honesty. Slumped on the warm leather couch, in front of the large window with panoramic views, I am suddenly keenly aware of my own smallness, weakness and lack of training. This is the ugly truth: I have not *made* myself into the kind of philosopher who can climb this level-sixteen wall. (To say nothing of actual mountains, with actual avalanches.)

And my paranoia about others watching me fail, or out-climbing me, is actually a distraction from my own flaws. Instead of concentrating on the wall, and my own ineptitude, I'm devoting attention to others' imagined judgement.

Importantly, the result of this realization is not paralysis, psychologically speaking – I still want to keep climbing. But I have a greater caution and reserve. I cannot simply hurl myself at the wall: I have to patiently judge my skills and fitness, and the layout of the wall and holds, and carefully try again.

Again, this is not a lesson reserved for vertical walls. Gravity in general is a stern teacher. Witness the gymnast's balance of humility and exertion. 'I will not fall again, I promised myself,' writes Comaneci. 'I fell again. I felt shame and stupidity . . . It was my first taste of failure, and I didn't like it at all.' Six years later, the Romanian gymnast scored the first perfect '10.00' at the Olympics. The beam, like the wall, humbled her – and, in doing so, helped her to improve.

Perhaps more prosaically (but no less importantly), I am humbled in the garage, as I add weight-plates to the bench press. I cannot pretend that, as I strain and fail to do ten repetitions, the steel 'has it in for me'. I simply do not have the muscles and stamina to count past eight. And if I want to add ten kilos more, this will require months of painful pushing and sweating. Again: I am not yet the philosopher who can bench-press eighty kilos.

In other words, in my humility, it is not God I am making room for, but ordinary reality: the stubborn facts of world and self. I cannot change the wall, but I can be more aware of its idiosyncrasies. I can also recognize my own muscles and talent, and my responsibility for leaving these uncultivated. This is what legendary Austrian mountaineer Heinrich Harrer, in *The White Spider*, referred to as a man's fight against 'his own weakness and insufficiency'.

Harrer was part of the historic 1938 climb of the Eiger's north face – an adventure that killed several young, fit and proficient climbers in the years before. Throughout his account of the climb, often undertaken in blinding snow, unstable ice and freezing storms, Harrer refers to the mindset required to climb the Eiger. He emphasizes not fear but uncertainty and diffidence. This is 'fear's friendly sister,' he writes, 'the right and necessary counterweight to that courage which urges men skywards, and protects them from self-destruction.'

Obviously Harrer was not a wallflower. No one climbs a killer mountain like the Eiger without ambition and passion – these were tough, eager young men, often raised in the mountains of Austria, Switzerland, Germany and Italy. They were pushed by what Harrer, with a touch of romanticism, calls 'the great adventure'. He was himself, he said, absurdly ambitious – unethically so, joining the Nazi party to get ahead. These men were also uncommonly fit: Harrer notes with approval the unyielding 'calf-muscles of the super-fit medical student who had grown up in the forests'.

Vigour and enthusiasm is why climbers need caution – they must be tempered by the 'diffidence' Harrer recommends. This is because rock climbing forces a confrontation between confidence and brute fact. A vertical wall cannot be flattered or intimidated. This is even more so for a real mountain: the Eiger, for example, with its icy traverses and freak storms – 'it offers no spur to one's courage,' writes Harrer, 'it simply threatens hard work and danger.' In the face of this, haste and conceit are a death sentence. The ascent – what Harrer calls 'the positive irruption in to the Vertical' – can be an education in candour. 'The glorious thing about mountains,' writes Harrer, 'is that they will endure no lies.'

The Eiger: a limestone lie detector.

Gymnastics, which *seems* far less dangerous than climbing, is equally brutal, and encourages a similar matter-of-factness. The beam or bars are indifferent to the gymnast; they cannot be bribed or coerced. Yet the gymnast jumps, somersaults, lifts and flips. This is why Comaneci's modesty was so valuable: it helped her to patiently, carefully accept the fundamental skills. 'Without the basics,' she writes in *Letters to a Young Gymnast*, 'a gymnast gets into danger – rips muscles, breaks bones, cracks vertebrae.' So the gymnast must put aside conceit and learn how to properly jump, spin, fall; must develop an attuned sense of her physical gifts *and* shortcomings, and how they relate to the equipment and space in front of her.

In other words, exercise often requires drive and excellent health, but also diffidence and intelligence: a willingness to dispassionately examine the situation and oneself, to assess calmly and act decisively. There is no room for misplaced pride when our fingers and spines are (literally) hanging in the balance. When we climb, leap or tumble, we develop a kind of practical humility: not frightened retreat from the world, but a more honest, careful congress with it.

Tip: Pride and humility can collaborate helpfully. Pride pushes on, humility pulls back – success requires both drive and caution.

Flow

Humility is all well and good, particularly when dangling from a clip screwed into thin, cracking vertical ice. But why climb a mountain in the first place? This is a question that applies to so many forms of exercise, including gymnastics, which seem to offer more humiliation and frustration than glory.

British mountaineer George Mallory, in reply to American journalists, gave a famous justification for scaling a mountain: 'Because it is there.' My seven-year-old son, Nikos, when asked why Harrer climbed the Eiger, was less gnomic: 'Because it's fun.' But neither explanation is convincing for us sensible grown-ups with sensible schedules that do not include falling insensibly from great peaks. 'With the best will in the world,' wrote Harrer in *The White Spider*, 'no one can inject a secret element of general usefulness to mankind into a climb of the Eiger's North Face.' The same might be said for ordinary rock and indoor climbing, and the beam or parallel bars: useless and painful. Football, tennis, cricket: they serve to move balls of various sizes from one spot to another, and tire us as they do. Surely all these exercises are pointless?

Yes, and this is partly why they are so valuable. Hungarian-born psychologist Mihaly Csikszentmihalyi calls rock climbing 'autotelic', but the word applies to most sports. Coming from the Greek for 'self' (*autos*) and 'purpose' (*telos*), a pursuit is autotelic when it is enjoyed for its own sake, not for the sake of something else. It might well end with praise, gifts or payment – Joe Simpson, author of the bestselling *Touching the Void*, for example, has made a career of his adventures. But he never climbed *for* money or popularity. He climbed (and almost died on) mountains in the Peruvian Andes because he delighted in 'immutable, anarchic living . . . simply being,' as he put it in *The Beckoning Silence*. Comaneci, who as a girl expected neither cash nor fame, suggests a similar elation: 'I was given the chance to run, climb, and soar, and loved it from the moment I entered the gym.'

What Simpson calls 'simply being' is described by Csikszentmihalyi as a 'flow' experience. Flow is a state of mind characterized by
feelings of freedom, loss of consciousness of self, and timelessness.
('Two more hours had slipped away,' said Harrer of his slow climb.)
In flow, the climber is aware of the mountain and himself – but this
is not always deliberate and calculating. Instead, consciousness is one
with the pursuit. 'When a climber is making a difficult ascent,' writes
Csikszentmihalyi in *Flow: The Psychology of Optimal Experience*, 'he is
totally taken up in the mountaineering role. He is 100 per cent a climber,
or he would not survive. There is no way for anything or anybody to
bring into question any other aspect of his self.' As in martial arts and
dance, this focus allows for skilled but spontaneous responses. The
leader of the Eiger climb, Anderl Heckmair, for example, was once
caught in a dangerous avalanche. In a matter of moments, he banged
in a piton, then protected it from the falling ice with his own (soon
flayed) hand. This intuitive response saved Heckmair's life where
conscious analysis and planning might have killed him.

Obviously Harrer, Simpson and their fellow mountaineers are
elite sportsmen. They see sport where others see granite. 'To most
people, the sheer wall of El Capitan in Yosemite Valley is just a huge
chunk of featureless rock,' writes Csikszentmihalyi. 'But to the
climber it is an arena offering an endlessly complex symphony of
mental and physical challenges.' Rock climbing has a variety of techniques, marking the novice from the competent – and the vocabulary
to go with them. ('I was crimping at the crux when I got Elvis leg.')
Similarly, my four-year-old daughter, Sophia, walking the beam at
the local municipal sports hall, is no Comaneci; my son, climbing a
peppercorn tree, is no Heckmair.

But for flow, we need not be elite or even highly proficient. It simply requires a match between skill and challenge. Too easy, and interest wanes. Too hard, and enjoyment is lost to confusion or anxiety. A novice like me will find difficulty in cement-rendered plywood and plastic; a Harrer or Simpson in a frozen, stormy rock, several thousand feet up. In *The Beckoning Silence*, Simpson wrote that the climber can be 'bored, intrigued, absorbed, alarmed, mentally certified and dead.' Flow begins with intrigue, arises with absorption, and responds rapidly to alarm. (As Heckmair's example suggests, it can also help to avoid the 'dead' part.) The point is to be mindfully engaged in an exercise that tests us.

This engagement also requires clear goals, which is why so many exercises and sports have continual scores or markers. For example, Harrer had to get to the top of the Eiger's north face, and down again. Each stage was recognized, and given a name: the Hinterstoisser Traverse, the Death Bivouac, the White Spider, for example. Comaneci had her set routines. And flow pursuits must have constant feedback to test progress. During the climb, Harrer tested his pitons and the depth of his ice picks, and continually felt the pull of gravity and gale. Likewise, Simpson wrote of 'the intricate mixture of power and subtlety,' he enjoyed while climbing Bridalveil Falls, 'the delicate balance between gymnastic dance and thuggish strength.'

We need not be exotic about this. For a child, climbing a tree might be a simple equivalent: a different scale of achievement, but requiring a similar combination of strength, flexibility, and feedback – for clear indicators of progress, one simply has to look down (or not). Likewise, the gymnast has a tactile and kinaesthetic sense of their body's movement in space. Speed, position, angle: the kick of the beam, the world spinning about one's centre, the balance of tension and timing as one's limbs stretch out. Tennis players are constantly aware of the court's lines, the movement of the ball, the opponent's strokes and the ongoing scores of the match – at each point, they have a sense of their position in the game. Exercise can provide us, in other words, with a clear destination, and a well-marked path. 'Flow' is all about enjoying the journey itself.

Tip: Flow does not require Olympic feats of adventure. Just try an exercise that challenges you and provides ongoing feedback of your progress.

But if physical exertion offers mental benefits, we have to be in the right frame of mind to enjoy this in the first place: hence the importance of humility. Flow is impossible without the recognition that we are fragile and flawed animals, navigating an indifferent or unstable environment. Precisely because of the stakes, the climber has to heed the rock's changing surfaces, the weather and altitude, her own body's flaws or potencies, her psychological blindspots and strengths. My son, when his calves and arms ache, must begrudgingly climb back down the tree – he is not yet strong enough to reach the top, and his diffidence is wise: a broken wrist or ankle means no more climbing.

Humility, in this, is a whole-person disposition: a willingness to see and feel our own failings, and how they relate to a challenging world. It does not make us meek. It helps us to enjoy challenges without paralysis or thoughtless bravado. It is a way to enlarge and enrich attention. The payoff is this very same attention: a quickened experience of skilful striving.

Mindfully engaged – in a peppercorn tree.

The point is not that we must be 'down on ourselves'– exercise does not mandate self-loathing. The point is that achievement requires a combination of ambition and failure. We have to be able to envisage difficult goals: aims that challenge our physical gifts and mental acuity. High, windswept peaks; multiple spins with a pinpoint landing; aces that just graze the inside of the fault line – they provide the tests that allow flow to arise.

But to enter this state of skilful engagement we also have to recognize our own insufficiency and imperfection. Even if we have the most refined talents – and most of us do not – we often have flaws of character: holes in attention, wayward emotions, fickle habits of perception. These will not be overcome abstractly, just by thinking about them. We have to do, fail, reflect on the task and our failure, and then do again. But we would not fail at all if it were not for the original ambition: the willingness to strive for something other than our customary aims.

Put another way, the humility of exercise is not simply a virtue of saints and holy men. Instead, it is a very human willingness to recognize that we are incomplete, and always will be, and that our attempts to remedy this existential shortfall will be enjoyable for their own sake, not because we will ever achieve perfection.

6. Pain

'Martial arts.' The words conjure up visions of Bruce Lee thwacking attackers with nunchakus, or Jason Statham in a black suit and thin tie, high-kicking a gang of nasties. The action-movie fantasy: the martial arts are about cruelty and suffering.

But actual martial arts, the stuff of ordinary men and women in white pyjamas, are often quite virtuous. Just as importantly, the martial arts demonstrate how pain in fitness can actually be enjoyed: as a reflection of our freedom. In karate, ballet or weights, pain we choose can actually be preferred to comfort without liberty.

Friendly Fighting

An early winter afternoon. I'm in my backyard with my friend Greg. Greg has an honours degree in philosophy and cultural studies, and works as a financial journalist. He knows about Chinese demand for potash. Greg lives with his girlfriend in an expensive inner-urban Melbourne suburb. He rows. His club's boats and oars are stored next to the clubhouses of Melbourne private schools. Greg is tall, well built, gregarious – safely roguish. Mothers like him.

I like Greg too. But this does not stop me punching him in the face.

It is a hooking right hand, which cracks Greg's cheek while my left traps his guard. He looks shocked. Then resolved.

I try to keep him away with jabs. It works at first. But I somehow throw out my elbow, and every punch ends with searing pain inside the joint. I try switching stances to lead with my right, but this is awkward.

Greg rushes me, guard up. I feel weak and small as he smacks me twice in the floating ribs. A ripping left hand, the knuckles still hard behind the glove's foam and leather. I wince and swing wildly at Greg's head. He moves cautiously away.

We start again, panting, and trying to avoid the kids' play equipment.

Afterwards, I have bruises all over my shoulders and chest. My left arm does not work properly for a few days. My ribs are tender. Greg's shoulder – recently reconstructed – clicks and throbs. His cheek is sore.

We agree to do it again soon. Greg refers to it as 'good fun', and I concur.

Virtue: It's a Knockout

Why are two middle-class, thirty-something writers hitting each other?

There are historical precedents. Ernest Hemingway, in his thirties, famously knocked poet Wallace Stevens into a puddle. Three times. But Greg was neither drunk, nor mocking my masculinity. (He knows how fragile it is.)

A more reasonable explanation: we were practising martial arts. But what *for*?

As a teenager, I was sent to karate to protect myself. In schoolyard scraps and the odd unfortunate street altercation, it worked: I kept

The journalist and the philosopher.

myself from being seriously harmed. (Scars notwithstanding.) And Greg has defended members of the public threatened by violence.

Yet we both now live in safe, affluent neighbourhoods, and work in relatively genteel middle-class professions. I am more likely to be discovered playing Lego with my children than throwing haymakers in a pub. Most of the violence I witness is symbolic: narrowed eyes at the supermarket checkout, as someone forgets to use the divider on the conveyor belt. Put simply, it is no longer to defend myself that I enjoy sparring: moving house or running away are far more likely to preserve my safety than headlocks and roundhouses.

Instead, I enjoy the martial arts because they are good for my character. They are, in a word, edifying. This is true for many martial artists, particularly in the so-called 'traditional' martial arts.

Importantly, there is evidence that this is not just slick advertising or Hollywood fantasy. As the psychological research reveals, martial artists are a peaceful cohort: more likely to avoid antisocial behaviour than to display it. In fact, several studies have demonstrated that participation in the fighting arts can actually make students less hostile. They become more confident, more willing to cooperate with others and less likely to entertain aggressive thoughts.

Education theorists call this 'skills transfer': what's learned in one domain is taken into another. For example, when I cross fists with Greg, who is taller, bigger and stronger, I am trying to be more brave. When I do so without being petty or malicious, I am trying to be more gregarious and restrained. When I am pummelled, I am trying to become more humble. At the same time, my aggressive urges are channelled into a safe, respectful environment, and combined with codes and rituals of conduct. I also confront my instincts of fear and

Sparring as a teenager: restraint for the victor, humility for me.

anger head on, instead of denying or celebrating them blithely – an exercise in self-awareness as well as self-control.

This provides a more reasonable explanation for my weekend backyard dust-up. The martial arts can help to cultivate virtues: pride, courage, moderation, sociability, for example. To take up karate, boxing or judo is to cultivate valuable social and psychological dispositions.

As it happens, the modern Japanese martial arts are called '*do*' for this very reason: it means 'way' or 'path'. *Do* refers to a way of living. Ju*do*, karate-*do*, aiki*do*: they are supposed to develop more civilized citizens, rather than simply more dangerous thugs. 'Skill is incidental,' wrote Jigoro Kano, the founder of judo. He believed that his martial art was chiefly training in a good life. The founder of Shotokan Karate, Gichin Funakoshi, wrote: 'Karate-do is not only the acquisition of certain defensive skills, but also the mastering of the art of being a good and honest member of society.' Likewise for many Chinese and Korean styles of fighting. And arts without commandments and moral handbooks – including boxing and mixed martial arts – can also be exercises in good conduct, particularly if the coaches or teachers provide an atmosphere of civility.

This is the answer to the seeming paradox of peaceful martial artists, thwacking one another in a school hall or backyard: training in violence can also be an education in the dispositions that help us avoid violence. The message of the film *The Karate Kid*, however twee, is basically right: the martial arts can be a lesson in virtue.

This lesson is important, because it points to the importance of context for exercise in general. Stepping onto the mat in a judo class is an acceptance of violence, a recognition that there will be throws and chokes. And not only violence, but competition: I will try to arm-lock my opponent, but not be pinned myself. The same logic underpins almost all competitive exercises: we are overt about our willingness to sprint faster, grow bigger muscles, jump higher bars.

In each case, the point is not to deny the more aggressive urges, but to give them a safe place to flourish. This weds impulse to achievement, and does so in an environment of relative safety. A punch in the karate school might have the same force and accuracy as a punch in a bar, but the former is thrown collaboratively, whereas the latter is an act of malice.

Put simply, exercise at its most virtuous is an enterprise of honesty: accepting the more destructive urges, and socializing them for the greater good.

Tip: Spend some time watching martial artists train. What looks like thuggery is often careful collaboration.

The Meaning of Pain

So the martial arts, even with their apparent brutality, can be virtuous. And likewise for other very physical sports. But why are they pleasurable? What is 'good fun', in Greg's words, about being punched in the ribs? Why do we speak of enjoying the 'burn' of weights training, or the strains and bruises of ballet? This is a tougher question.

It also seems like a nonsensical question. Even a cursory look at the martial arts make one thing clear: they necessitate pain and injury. In most amateur sports, pain is usually incidental and accidental. We might be tripped in football or netball. We might have sore quadriceps after sprinting, and aching biceps after curls. But these games or exercises do not *require* pain and injury in the same way. We might lift weights, for example, without the agony of the professional bodybuilder.

Whereas the martial arts, to be genuinely martial – that is, to help us defend ourselves – are immediately and regularly threatening. The exercises themselves involve some bodily violation. In judo, we are thrown. In karate, we are punched and kicked. In Brazilian ju-jitsu, we are choked.

In this, the martial arts involve an extreme version of the pain endured in many other exercises. They provide a handy test case: if we can explain the enjoyment of karate elbows or judo reaps, we can certainly do so for weights training or dance.

At first blush, there is nothing 'fun' about feeling pain, as Greg's comment might suggest. But this is not quite true, and it all hinges on the word 'feeling'. Feelings are actually two quite different things: sensations and emotions. The first is the feeling *of* something. The second is how I feel *about* it.

For example, the sensation of a gloved punch to the ribs is quite similar to other knocks: tripping over my son's Lego dragon and falling onto the arm of the couch, for instance. Both involve a hard edge (bone or wood) with a soft covering (foam or upholstery) smacking into my midsection. The sensations are alike: an acute sharp pain, then a dull, tender ache for hours. Yet falling onto the couch concludes with angry muttering and a dark mood, whereas Greg's punches end with comradely banter.

And this is not simply macho posturing. Women enjoy fighting too. Witness Leah Hager Cohen, in *Without Apology: Girls, Women and the Desire to Fight*:

On the canvas, it was fun – fun with a narrow eye and an edge, with rasping lungs and a slamming heart, and legs now tiring, going rubbery – but fun like I was unaccustomed to: fun incarnate. Everything, even colours, seemed more vibrant.

While the martial arts have a unique relationship to pain, other exercises can leave us equally comfortable with discomfort. Like many white-collar workers, I dedicate plenty of free hours to picking up and putting down heavy lumps of iron, and pushing myself up off the floor (then down, then up, then down). As I do, I hurt: from aches and searing pinches, to muscle tremors and overall malaise. I run up hills until I want to retch. Yet, as I sit here at a stuffy cafe on a Saturday morning, I look back on the bench-presses and push-ups with easy fondness. I prefer the agony of exertion to this muggy, monolithic comfort.

Ballet, while not strictly an exercise or sport, is equally known for its transformation of agony into art. Karen Kain, ballerina with Canada's National Ballet, told CBC of waking up with ankles like glass, 'like they might shatter when I walked on them. And that's what they feel like just about every morning.' For many dancers, pain is not something to be avoided at all costs, but an ordinary part of the artistic endeavour – something to shrug at, not lament. Yoko van der Tweel, from the Dutch National Ballet, told researcher Anna Aalten about her relationship to pain:

When you are dancing you do not feel any pain. Once, during a rehearsal one of my *pointe* shoe ribbons broke. I put it together with a safety pin and while I was dancing the pin

started to bend and the point of it went through my foot. This
had been going on for some time and the bleeding was heavy.
But I did not feel a thing! Because I had been dancing and
concentrating on the dancing. Therefore you do not feel pain
in that situation.

This is not simply a matter of putting the pain to one side; of grinning and bearing it. It is that the ballerina does not *have* to bear it.
With her professional training and dedication to the dance, the cut
is simply not felt *as* a cut. As with martial arts, ballet can change the
meaning of pain. And, as meaning changes, so does the pain itself.

Modern work in psychology and medicine confirms this idea
of changeable pain. One of the leading experts on pain is Canadian
psychologist Ronald Melzack. Melzack's work with patients suffering
'phantom limb' pains led him to reject what he calls 'Descartes' speci-
ficity theory' of pain. For Descartes, as we have seen, the body was
basically a machine. It was not fused with the mind, but made of a
separate substance. So pain was a purely mechanical process of stimulation and transmission. The brain's job, as a thinking substance,
was simply to receive it.

Melzack's work revealed that this picture was all wrong. The mind
and body are intimately interconnected, and there are no mechanical
laws of feeling. The physical make-up of our nervous system allows for
great variation in pain, depending on mood, memory and attention.

The nerve impulses from my punched ribs, for example, do not
run straight to my mind. They pass through what Melzack calls a
'spinal gating mechanism' in the dorsal horn, which is in the spinal
cord. This mechanism is influenced by the brain, which sends

Painless en pointe: ballerina Karen Kain with Denys Ganio in *Carmen*.

signals to thick and thin fibres in the 'gateway': activity in the thick fibres tend to close it, thin fibres open it. Only *some* stimuli become what I recognize as 'pain'.

The upshot of Melzack's theory is that pain is not a raw stimulus. It is a pattern of activity in the brain, in response to the world, including our 'inner world': ideals, values, fantasies, memories. 'Stimuli might trigger the patterns,' writes Melzack, 'but do not produce them.' Pain is shaded by our mind, which is itself coloured by complex psychological and social influences.

In other words, I do not simply feel Greg's punch as pain, then interpret it as 'fun'. The sensation *itself* is changed by my mental state, including my emotions, but also my ideas of myself and perceptions of others, by my recollections of the past and expectations for the future. 'The force behind a punch is very subjective,' writes Australian author and champion boxer Mischa Merz, author of *Bruising* and *The Sweetest Thing*. 'What would have bothered me a couple of years earlier to the point of panic had become a mere irritation.' Likewise for van der Tweel's safety pin: within the craft of the dance, it is not felt at all.

Put simply, what hurts is part of the whole project of my life – as the project changes, so does the pain. In particular, pain becomes preferable when it is freely accepted. As we saw, I am far angrier about cracking my torso on the couch than I am about my friend's violence. Greg was deliberately punching me, his friend, and yet my fury was reserved for inanimate furniture. The difference was not in the pain itself: its amount, location or combination of sharpness and dullness. The difference was what it *meant*. One was a known risk, which was consented to. The other was an inadvertent bit of (sadly) characteristic clumsiness.

Confession: I once gave myself a black eye during a schoolyard wrestling match. Clumsiness has been a lifelong companion.

My Pain

In other words, pleasurable pain signifies freedom: that I have *chosen* to put myself at risk. This does not mean I want to be hurt. Quite the contrary: I will do everything in my power to avoid getting round-housed and wristlocked. But this 'power' is exactly the point: I am committing to sparring because I believe my skills, fitness and virtues will keep me from serious harm. This requires trust in my opponent, and – in a school – in the teacher, coach or referee. But it also requires trust in myself: that I will strive and endure. Likewise for weights training (no one forces me to load up the curl bar) and dance. 'You are the one who wants to be here, if you don't like it you can leave,' paraphrases ballerina Nienke Bonnema, about the culture of pain in her art. 'So you simply did not dare to stop, you just went on.'

In some cases, this attitude leads to injury: torn muscles during curls, bulging cervical discs from throws, and damaged knuckles from pointe.

But for most amateurs, exercising for a more balanced life, the result is a healthy refusal to treat pain as something automatically terrifying. Pain, in this, is no longer a sign of foolishness or power-lessness. It signifies a kind of autonomy: it is *my* pain.

This is valuable, because irritation is ubiquitous in life. Whether it is psychological (the stress of a book behind deadline) or physio-logical (haemorrhoids from sitting writing a book behind deadline), every commitment in professional and domestic life asks for some discomfort, at some point. While jobs, schooling or parenting might not demand strained muscles or black eyes, they certainly take their metaphorical pound of flesh. The pain of exercise is helpful, because it reminds us of what liberty looks like: the agony or injury that we choose and, in so choosing, consecrate. The same question then remains for career, relationship or education: is this what I want, and how willing am I to suffer for it?

In other words, pain is a test of value: it sharpens our perception of what is worthwhile in life, and just what we are willing to sacrifice to get it. Exercise, precisely because of its discomfort, is a touchstone for an emancipated existence.

7. Consistency

Haruki Murakami was a jazz-bar owner, serving spirits at odd hours. He smoked a hundred cigarettes a day. Now he is Japan's bestselling novelist, who runs marathons. (And goes to bed early.)

Murakami's balance of writing and running reveals the intellectual value of strength and stamina: how so-called 'mental' work is also unavoidably physical. It also demonstrates the existential rewards of regular exercise: a life of greater integrity and constancy. Weekly sessions at the gym, or on the footpath, can help us to avoid 'losing the plot'.

At Least He Never Walked

The year is 1983. Duran Duran are on radio rotation. And Japanese novelist Haruki Murakami is jogging, topless and sunburnt, along a Greek highway. Not just any highway: Marathon Avenue, which runs from Athens to the famous town of Marathon, where the Athenians defeated the Persians in 490 BC. There are no Persians on the road: just the corpses of three dogs and eleven cats.

While prudent Greeks are heading home for siesta, Murakami is running a marathon – running *the* Marathon (albeit backwards). It is midsummer, and locals have dubbed his run 'insane'. But he keeps his word: twenty-five miles in the dry heat. He starts early, but the sun is soon blinding and blistering. Murakami cannot stop drinking. He fantasizes about ice-cold beer. His skin is white with salt.

As he nears the village of Marathon, Murakami gets grumpy: at the press photographer in the van, taking snaps for the newspaper; at his editor, cheerfully egging him on; at the sheep munching grass ('Who needs this many sheep, anyway?').

After almost four hours of jogging, sweating and stinging, Murakami reaches his finish line. He wants to sprint, but cannot. 'All my muscles,' he writes, 'feel like they've been shaved away with a rusty plane.' He slowly completes his marathon, gulps down his (anticlimactic) beer, and then rests contented. 'Whew! – I don't have to run anymore.'

Until the next race, that is. Haruki Murakami has run a marathon almost every year, for the past quarter of a century. (He missed one race because of illness. That year he competed in a triathlon.) While training in Hawaii and Cambridge, Massachusetts, he ran at least thirty-six miles a week, six days a week. He ran in every season; ran in Mediterranean sunshine, Boston mist-rain, New York headwinds; ran when busy, stressed, injured. He competed in an ultramarathon in Japan: over sixty miles of foot-slogging madness, which ended with the novelist on 'autopilot', cruising robotically to the finish line. Toward the end of his book *What I Talk About When I Talk About Running*, he gives his own epitaph: 'At Least He Never Walked.'

Confession: I jog regularly, but my longest run is just under nine miles. It takes me an hour and twenty minutes. Murakami, over twenty years my senior, ran seven times that distance in under twelve hours.

Not just about beer: Boston Marathon, 1980.

Reveries and Strength

Why does Murakami do it? In each case, his daily slog is intimately related to his day job: writing. In other words, his physical exertion has mental benefits.

First off, Murakami enjoys the psychological 'idleness' that jogging brings. This is not to say that his mind is completely vacant. He thinks about the weather, happy or sad events, the odd stray memory. He also thinks about the run, the end of the run and its scenery: beer and pretty blonde joggers, for example. ('Without pleasures like that,' he writes, 'it's pretty hard to get up and go jogging every morning.') He argues with himself and his body, trying to stop pain, exhaustion or anxiety. But, as we saw earlier, his thoughts just come and go, with no obvious logic. This is runner's reverie, the 'transient hypofrontality' we saw with Darwin. And like the grandfather of evolutionary theory, Murakami the novelist enjoys this in solitude.

Running also keeps Murakami fit and strong, which is vital for writing. It might seem absurd to link *Norwegian Wood* with physical fitness, but its author is adamant: he names 'endurance' as one of a writer's key qualities. Writing is certainly a mental pursuit, which requires thought, reflection, recollection, imagination. But crafting a book is not something that only happens 'inside' the mind. The whole body is involved in the creative endeavour: sitting for hours, scribbling at a notebook, refusing the legs' restlessness; stomach aches as anxiety releases acid; headaches and stinging eyes from sitting staring at white pages or screens two feet away. And the brain itself requires energy: it cannot concentrate for hours every day, for months or years, without taking a toll. 'You might not move your body around,' writes Murakami, 'but there's a gruelling, dynamic labour going on inside you.'

Question: Are you ever exhausted by so-called 'mental' work? If so, just how 'mental' is it?

It is no coincidence that Murakami's exercise regime began alongside his career as an author. Once a chain-smoking bar owner with odd hours and a poor diet, Murakami took up writing and jogging almost simultaneously. 'If I wanted to have a long life as a novelist,' he says, 'I needed to find a way to keep fit and maintain a healthy weight.' Jogging was simple, required no training or equipment, and suited his daily routines. It also encouraged him to eat more healthily: fewer doughnuts, more fresh fruit and vegetables, and lean fish.

Put simply, running was a way for Murakami to relax and refine his mind, and bolster his writing body.

We need not run in the Greek sun to gain this strength. A good session on a treadmill has the same benefits for blood flow; a daily trip up and down the stairwell is also toughening. And, as not everyone can have a novelist's working hours, it helps to choose exercises that can be done in lunch breaks, or after work: in a gym nearby, or around the block when the weather allows. Minnesotan author David Lebedoff often jogs on a treadmill in his basement when snowed in. Lebedoff writes:

> Running indoors is much better than not running at all. A large indoor track is just fine. Well, it's better than the cold-weather alternative, which is the treadmill. This is very

boring, not to mention being a scary metaphor, but it does get the heart pumping, which gets the mind working, which keeps the keyboard humming.

Even ultramarathon runner Dean Karnazes, who becomes woefully depressed without jogging ('relaxing for me is really stressful') has run on a treadmill. (Of course, he ran on a treadmill for two days non-stop, until his toenails fell off.) The point is not to break records or write a masterpiece. The point is to keep training the body to best support the mind; to enhance the organs of labour. If we are thinking beings, we are also beings with bodies – bodies with organs and muscles, including brains, which thrive with blood and flexing.

Tip: If you are an office worker, exercise is not simply an antidote to stress or sedentary living. It is a training for the labour of work itself. It can help concentration, problem-solving skills and energy levels.

How to Not Lose the Plot

But there are more subtle benefits to exercising regularly, whatever the weather, whatever our mood. And they come from the very fact *of* exercising regularly. When Murakami drags himself from bed and laces up his plain Mizuno running shoes ('the Subaru of the shoe world,' says the author), he is practising the virtues of integrity and constancy.

Why is this important? In his landmark 1984 book *After Virtue*, philosopher Alasdair MacIntyre argued that the modern age has lost a crucial idea of what it is to live a whole life. Lives, he said, are not random collections of moments, not dust piles made of scattered clumps. They are unities.

To make sense of Murakami's running, for example, it is not enough to see him on the asphalt. We also have to know of his nicotine-stained past in the hospitality industry, his present juggle of writing and jogging, and his hopes for the future: health, his next opus, next year's marathon. And each jog is also a unity. From starting buzz to mid-race frailty to final exhilaration: no moment makes sense on its own.

This is why MacIntyre argued that lives are actually narratives. This is the stuff of human existence: beginnings, middles, ends; departures and destinations; courtships, arousals and climaxes. 'Stories are lived,' wrote MacIntyre, 'before they are told – except in the case of fiction.' Obviously they are not just made up, as Murakami might invent his protagonists. We are at best 'co-authors' of our lives.

To live a good life, says MacIntyre, these stories have to be pulled together *as* wholes. We easily become fractured, divided, conflicted. We can 'lose the plot', so to speak. This is why we need the virtues of integrity and constancy. Integrity is achieved in changing circumstances; constancy over changing times. Both character traits are tendencies towards wholeness: virtues of consistency, which pull our stories together.

These stories then help us to negotiate and navigate life's problems by providing a meaningful framework. They cannot magically turn random pain into joy, but they can put failure and accident into perspective. Narratives can reveal ongoing biases, common tensions, dogged ambitions – they help to alleviate the anxiety that comes with contradiction and ambiguity, and can nudge us to reconcile parts of ourselves usually in conflict. 'When someone complains . . . that his or her life is meaningless,' writes MacIntyre, 'he or she is often . . . complaining that the narrative of their life has become unintelligible to them, that it lacks any point'. The virtues of consistency cannot give life a purpose, but they help to pull our lives together *towards* some purpose.

Regular exercise is a version of this lived unity: a commitment to consistency, despite the vicissitudes of life. Murakami, for example, is a successful author, with all the duties this brings. In 2005, while writing *What I Talk About When I Talk About Running*, he is busy: doing publicity for a new collection of short stories, revising translations of Raymond Carver, checking proofs and covers for a book of criticism, looking for a new assistant, writing lectures. No doubt he is also writing a new novel. But he still runs every day. He is not just a writer or a runner – he has pledged himself to both. He has to be clear about his commitments, and to keep meeting them in 1983 or 2005, in Boston and Japan. 'If I used being busy as an excuse not to run,' he writes, 'I'd never run again.'

Author David Lebedoff makes the same point:

There are plenty of places to run. The first is called outside. If you're still looking for excuses you can say that running on sidewalks is bad for your feet and knees. The answer to this is not to run on sidewalks. Even in the most highly urbanized places there is plenty of open ground. Honestly. Look at a map. Ask a friend.

Just as importantly for Murakami, writing and running have a common logic: between drive and rest, flexibility and rigidity,

Murakami stretching . . . himself.

inwardness and worldliness, confidence and doubt. In each case, Murakami's jogging helps him to regulate his daily life; to find the balance between competing impulses. What the author achieves on the footpath, he uses on the page. 'Most of what I know about writing I've learned through running every day,' he writes. 'These are practical, physical lessons.' In this light, jogging is not only a symbol of MacIntyre's consistent life, but also a tool for maintaining it.

Current research cautiously confirms Murakami's ideas. A study by psychologists Megan Oaten and Ken Cheng, from Sydney's Macquarie University, suggests that mental strength echoes physical strength. They argue that self-regulation – our ability to override or guide unwanted impulses – is something like a 'muscle'. Used intensely and at length, it gets weaker: we sit instead of walking, eat junk food instead of lean whole foods. But training can make the muscle of self-regulation stronger. It still gets tired, but not as quickly, and not for as long.

And, more vitally, self-regulation can be trained by exercise, like Murakami's running. In Oaten and Cheng's study, exercise enabled participants to control their urges more effectively, and not just at the gym: they ate healthier food, smoked less, drank less coffee, were on time more often and left fewer filthy dishes in the sink. They were also in a better mood.

The cheerier and more consistent exercisers were not elite athletes. They were ordinary students, some no doubt juggling casual work, study and chores with trips to the local gym. This is also true of other writers, like David Lebedoff, who balances writing with his day job as an attorney. Like many in the northern hemisphere, Lebedoff spends part of his winter travelling from home, to car, to garage, to heated office, and back again – no Mediterranean marathons in Minnesota, 'where global warming is celebrated', as Lebedoff puts it. His trips to the basement treadmill are hardly exotic, and sometimes dull. But he keeps up the routine because these sessions, always undertaken while juggling several vocational and domestic balls, encourage him to be more reliable. 'The fact that it takes character to get out of your chair,' he writes, 'is perhaps the greatest benefit to be derived from exercise.'

These are exactly the kinds of virtues MacIntyre recommends: traits of a whole life, not just here or there. Exercise does not simply make Murakami a better sportsman or writer, by enriching his mind or enhancing his stamina. It also strengthens his 'muscles' of constancy and integrity, so his grasp of his own character is firmer for longer. 'A writer has a quiet, inner motivation,' writes Murakami, 'and doesn't seek validation in the outwardly visible.' Replace 'writer' with 'runner' and the meaning is the same: an exercise in a tightly plotted life. And this is not restricted to bestselling authors. By making us less fatigued by self-regulation, exercise provides us with the faculties for a more consistent life story. It is training in becoming whole.

'Because of the Pain'

Constancy and integrity ask for a little suffering. Sore leg muscles, anxiety over race times, morning weariness: Murakami is quite clear about the agony and annoyances of regular jogging. And he *needs* his running to be painful and exhausting. Not because of some maso-chistic longing for torture – well, not only – but because consistency is best cultivated by confronting what is *not* pleasant. 'No animal in its right mind,' writes Death Valley ultramarathon champion Pam Reed, 'would undertake such a thing. That's the point, of course. [It] is all about going against your instincts.'

We have already seen the way pain becomes pleasure as its meaning changes. In this case, pain adds to consistency by challenging us to maintain consistency and integrity. Consistency would be pointless if life were uncomplicated and unconflicted; if all we needed were good intentions. But we are often torn between competing roles and priorities, with depleted time and energy. We can, in other words, easily lose the plot. By committing to constant exercise, which is draining and painful, we are developing habits of wholeness in spite of all this. 'It's precisely because of the pain, precisely because we want to overcome that pain,' writes Murakami, 'that we can get the feeling . . . of really being *alive* – or at least a partial sense of it.' David Lebedoff, sweating in the basement or walking around one of Minneapolis's lakes, makes a similar point. 'The really hard steps are the first ones,' he writes. 'Not the first running steps – even those are enjoyable – but rather the impossibly difficult task of getting ready to run. If just getting out of the chair seems difficult, then you *really* need to do so.'

By overcoming pain and tiredness, we are making a commitment to our own consistency, because it is easy to give up when aching or weak. And we are doing so again and again, because this is what virtues are: habits, not just abstract ideas. This is why Murakami ran in Greece's baking summer: not because dehydrating burns more calories (sports medicine suggests otherwise), but because he had committed to the Marathon labour. Murakami writes:

I didn't start running because somebody asked me to become a runner. Just like I didn't become a novelist because someone asked me to. One day, out of the blue, I wanted to write a novel. And one day, out of the blue, I started to run – simply because I wanted to. I've always done whatever I felt like doing in life.

Running, like writing, is part of *his* story, which the author will live doggedly, and keep living when things (inevitably) get tough. Likewise for each of us, panting on the footpath or basement treadmill, or doing maddeningly dull curls at the local gymnasium: we are affirming ourselves by meeting discomfort head on.

Tip: Running intelligently does not mean injury, but it often means pain or exhaustion. Without challenge, no virtues are required to finish.

Lugging Around the Suitcase of the Self

How competitive do we need to be? Murakami is certainly driven to succeed: witness his profound humiliation while hobbling to the finish line in the Chiba marathon, his limbs frozen by ocean winds ('I never, ever wanted to go through that again'). But his chief competitor is time, not other runners – and time will not stop for him. Because of this, Murakami keeps pushing himself to run faster, longer, steeper.

But as he ages, the author's times get poorer, regardless of how he trains. Yes, ultramarathon runners in their forties and fifties can beat twenty-somethings. But time's arrow points one way, and the target isn't youth. 'How pitiful and pointless this shabby little container called *me* is,' Murakami writes. This recognition, gained from his daily foot slog, is not a cause for cynicism. Merely an acknowledgement of the obvious facts: Murakami *is* ageing, weaker, slower. But he keeps on. It's a groping drive for continuity, which he compares to 'lugging around that old suitcase'. He is his own baggage. 'Athletes are inherently competitive people,' writes Pam Reed. 'Ultimately, though, you compete against yourself.'

So exercising regularly can certainly be training in high ambitions: a stubborn refusal to give up, despite the pain. But its benefits are those of maturity, not youthful urgency: patience, fortitude and the avoidance of caprice. We succeed, not always by increasing our speeds, scores or weights, but by dealing regularly with discomfort and failure, in the interests of a consistent character. The point is not that competition is to be avoided. The point is that the prize of striving – against others, or for a personal best – is a greater capacity to strive, and to make sense of this endeavour, win or lose.

8. The Sublime

The beach or pool can be scenic backdrop or promenade: somewhere to see, or be seen.

But the water can also be a chance to savour the sublime: a joyful fear, which suggests danger alongside security. It also evokes oneness: a rejoining with the world. In this, the sublime is a reminder of our human condition: divided from things, yet thrown amongst them gainfully.

Boats and Submarines

My first memory of the sea: slugs and snails inside my wellingtons. Actually, my boots were full of sand and water, but to my pre-school mind the gritty squelch was because of slimy gastropods, crawling into my shoes. My lesson: the water is indifferent to seams, borders and barriers. It invades us, as we invade it.

Aged about six, I stood at Noosa beach in subtropical Queensland, grinning as the warm sea frothed at my ankles. Then suddenly I was on my face, sand in my gap-toothed mouth, hacking up a lung while the waves pushed me over and over. Another lesson: the water is not kidding around.

At primary school, my father tried to teach me to 'swim like a boat' at the local pools. I answered that I was a submarine, and stayed underwater, looking at the strange world of doubly rippled adult bodies: folds of fat and skin warped by waves from older kids jumping in the deep end. I loved the way the pools' chaos – kids' screams, splashes, parental monologues about food and stitches – was muted by the water. Everything became a warm, fuzzy, blue-green noise.

I learned to be a boat, but the submariner remained. The water, for me, was always something to be *in*, not simply above. It was more a site of secular pilgrimage than a thoroughfare.

As a teenager, I spent weeks on end at the beach. I usually swam to the third reef of our local cove, marked by a high wooden pole stuck with mussels. To me, this marked the end of the beach and the start of the bay: the sand below dropped away. At this point, dry land was suddenly absurd – the whole world was waves, blurry blacknesses and solitude.

For hours, I floated and looked: at the unsettling, unnameable *nothing* of it all. Translucent, eerily quiet, a monolith of constant movement, the sea always suggested more than I saw. Treading water in fogged goggles, a tiny little hairless mammal without gills, dorsal fins or blowhole, I was scared and never happier.

What was I seeking in the pool and sea? I had no word for this waterlogged bliss. There was nothing in baffling differential equations, Public Enemy albums or Atari ST computer games – to name my teenaged pursuits – that resembled this feeling of fearful joy. Perhaps English literature, which I studied absent-mindedly in year 11, might have suggested the word: swimming in the sea was *sublime*.

Question: What are your first memories of the sea and swimming? Can you remember when paddling became swimming? How did this feel?

The author in 1984, begrudgingly becoming a boat.

An Agreeable Kind of Horror

The notion of the sublime was most popular in the eighteenth and nineteenth centuries. While the ideas varied, the sublime was summed up neatly by English author Joseph Addison, recently returned from his Grand Tour. 'You have a near prospect of the Alps, which are broken into many steps and precipices,' he wrote in *Remarks on Several Parts of Italy, &c*, 'that they fill the mind with an agreeable kind of horror.' In short: the sublime requires both enjoyment *and* fear.

Irish statesman and scholar Edmund Burke, writing half a century later, saw the ocean as an exemplary case of this sublime. The sea, argued Burke in *A Philosophical Enquiry into the Origin of Our Ideas of the Sublime and the Beautiful*, often inspires dread. Most obviously, the sea is immense. Even smaller bays swallow up the swimmer, suggesting a kind of infinity: a greatness that dwarfs the body and boggles the mind. Tom Farber, in *On Water*, calls it 'that vastness where whales would be nothing in the vastness.' The sea is often obscure, too: from a frothy bay thick with sand and kelp, to deep ocean reefs where light is dim, our eyes are hampered. The water's silence achieves the same ambiguity: a muffled world we cannot quite fathom. 'The old round of life and death,' writes Jacques Cousteau, 'passes silently.' And not only the sea – David Allan Evans, in his short story 'The Celebration', described the 'private, cold, and muddy darkness' of a rural lake. Even if the water is obviously safe, the murkiness works on the mind to imply dangerous or uncanny vastness. 'A clear idea,' wrote Burke, 'is . . . another name for a little idea.' And little ideas do not frighten.

Burke also noted power's role in the sublime: the sea's energy is straightforwardly dangerous. We can drown in a cup of water, but the sea has strong waves and sharp rocks, which overpower strong swimmers and rip skin. 'In rough ocean, I have thrown up from beginning to end of a thirteen-hour swim,' wrote long-distance swimmer Diana Nyad, 'swishing around like a cork . . . I would do anything to stop this feeling – and the only thing that will is to be on dry land.' The sea is also capricious in this, moving from mirror calm to violent storm in minutes. In short, we are never really in charge. 'Wheresoever we find strength, and in what light soever we look upon power,' wrote Burke, 'we shall all along observe the sublime'. The point is not that the sea actually does drown or cut us, but that we know it *can*, and that we are too weak to stop it. The sublime always requires some hint of danger and pain.

In fact, water in general can suggest danger and annihilation, because we are not well adapted to aquatic life. (Michael Phelps's top sprinting speed is about a third of a dolphin's.) Breathing is hampered as we swim. Studies suggest that the water compresses the chest, making it more difficult to inhale. While floating horizontally takes pressure off breathing muscles, blood pools in the lungs, leaving less room for oxygen. In freestyle, we also burn more energy for less oxygen, because of the short, over-the-shoulder breaths – what poet Maxine Kumin, in '400-meter freestyle', calls 'little sips carefully expended'. As a result, our lungs tire more quickly during swimming than during exercises like running or rowing – in a matter of minutes we suffer what researchers call 'inspiratory fatigue'. This, in turn, leaves us with less air in our lungs, and oxygen in our cells. This then has flow-on effects for the whole body: our muscles become weaker or slower, and have more trouble coordinating.

And when swimming, we are also using more muscle groups. Swimming is called 'low impact' because it supports the body while it works – no thumping the asphalt with feet. But it is a particularly taxing exercise. Stomach, chest, upper and lower back, shoulders, biceps and triceps, and the upper and lower legs, including the feet: all working in a coordinated and continuous way to keep the swimmer from stopping and sinking. American Olympic champion Don Schollander, who won four gold medals in 1964, described the pain in his biography *Deep Water*:

> It begins, coming on gradually, hitting your stomach first. Then your arms grow heavy and your legs tighten – thighs first, then knees. You sink lower in the water . . . as though someone were pushing down on your back.

Put simply, even the local pool can suggest danger, by highlighting the continual effort required to simply keep our head above water. Swimming, whether in salt water or chlorine, evokes the sublime by revealing just how vulnerable we are.

How does this work? Burke's explanation was matter-of-fact. He argued that dangers – implied or real – required bodily effort. To respond to a seething or darkly deep sea was to exercise the nervous system, leading to a kind of alert relaxation – what Burke called 'tranquility tinged with horror'. Taking in a boundless ocean, for example, taxed the eye muscles and retina. Looking at wave after wave aroused the eyes, causing a 'vibration' that was tiring but exhilarating. 'Being violently aroused by this continued agitation,' the eye, wrote Burke, 'presents the mind with a grand or sublime conception.' Sudden changes in vision or sound, like an ocean storm or freezing water, increased tension, which was frightening but exhilarating. Even darkness had a physical explanation: the iris of the eye, straining as it dilated, left one calmly invigorated.

Burke's ideas might seem absurd, but he was right to seek physical explanations. Contemporary neuroscience cannot give a complete picture of the sublime, but some studies are suggestive. For example, English art historian John Onians reports that challenging or chaotic situations cause our brains to work harder. Information from the retina – the receptive 'screen' at the back of the eye – normally follows a regular path: recognition, recollection and response, for example. But when we see something unusual or unexpected, like a foaming, translucent sea, the brain involves more neuronal areas and connections – what Onians calls 'mental movement'. We are used to pictures of the sea, or brief glimpses between buildings – the sea can become a simple, pretty bit of scenery. But that first view of the immense rippling horizon, or rushing dive into the water, can briefly set the brain labouring. As Burke noted, this abruptness can also evoke the sublime. This is the hallucinatory buzz captured by Carol Anshaw in her novel *Aquamarine*, as she jumps into a pool: 'The next minute is an aquamarine blur. The colour shatters into a million wavy panes as the water prisms the sunlight that hits the bottom.'

Even when not confusing or surprising, the water can also encourage the secretion of norepinephrine, which ups heart rate, triggers glucose release and gets our muscles ready to respond. This is not only useful for survival, but also stimulating. 'Several of these reactions are ones that make us feel more alert and engaged,' writes Onians, 'and so make us feel good.' This is evoked by Jack London's breathless prose in his story 'The Kanaka Surf', as he describes a couple body-surfing: 'side by side, and six feet apart . . . they dived straight under the over-curl even then disintegrating to chaos and falling.' Tim Winton describes this same battered exhilaration in young West Australian surfers. 'The back was out of his wetsuit and there was skin off his shoulders,' Winton writes in *Breath*. 'His nose bled, his legs trembled, but by the time Sando reached us he was laughing.'

The point is not that the sublime can be reduced to neurones and neurotransmitters. The point is that swimming, because of water's unique properties, suggests stimulating potency. This is different to the 'flow' we saw in climbing and gymnastics, in which pain or danger direct our awareness. These feelings allow 'flow' to arise, by fixing attention on what's vital for success or survival. With the sublime, feelings of discomfort and threat *are* the feeling – they are enjoyed as part of the encounter with power. The water's fluidity, size, and power encourage a vulnerable aliveness.

Does this mean we have to drive to the roughest, most treacherous beaches to savour the sublime? No, Burke argued: there is no enjoyment of the sublime without safety. Being picked up by a wave and dumped on sharp mussel shells is not blissful – it simply hurts. Swimming too far and becoming lost provides no joy – it is just terrifying. The sublime comes from the passions of survival, without the desperate need *to* survive. 'When danger or pain press too nearly, they are incapable of giving any delight, and are simply terrible,' wrote Burke, 'but at certain distances, and with certain modifications, they may be . . . delightful.' In other words, the sublime sea is best enjoyed by a strong swimmer in the surf, or a weak swimmer in the shallows or pool.

Tip: *The sublime does not require elite athletic swimming, just some hint of danger or pain. A child may get this from a simple beach visit, a weak swimmer from a calm pool. The point is to enjoy the power and size of the water.*

That 'Oceanic' Feeling

The German philosopher Arthur Schopenhauer, writing in *The World as Will and Idea*, added to this portrait of the swimming sublime: it involves a feeling of oneness. Schopenhauer described a storm at sea, with 'waves, high as houses . . . driven violently against steep cliffs.' Anyone watching this is profoundly aware that they are, as Schopenhauer put it, 'an infinitesimal dot in relation to stupendous powers'. This is not a feeling reserved for nineteenth-century scholars. 'I seemed to shrink and shrink,' wrote Australian swimmer Annette Kellerman, 'till I was nothing but a flecky bubble and feared that the bubble would burst.'

Yet at the same moment the beach-goer feels tiny and powerless, argued Schopenhauer, they also feel 'eternal, tranquil.' To illustrate this, Schopenhauer introduced the idea of the night sky, with its 'countless worlds'. His idea was that, in reflecting on the infinity of blackness and stars, we recognize that all the universe's details are our own invention – the categories of selfish minds trying to survive. The real cosmos is a great whole and we are parts of it; we are, as Schopenhauer put it, 'exalted by its immensity.'

We do not have to commit to the German's philosophy to explain his 'exultation'. The oneness of the snorkeller does not simply arise

On the edge of infinity (with bucket).

from reflection; from some otherworldly meditation. We are literally *in* the sea or pool. Our skin, even in a wetsuit, is constantly in contact with the water. Of course this is true of the air too – only astronauts escape into a vacuum. But we do not normally *feel* the air. Whereas the water clings to us; every part of our skin registers this thin presence: cool, flowing, heavy. 'I love to throw myself into the sea,' wrote Sharon Olds in her poem 'The Swimmer', 'cold fresh enormous palm around my scalp.'

Importantly, this grip does not stop us paddling, kicking, diving – the water is somewhat hospitable, displaced by our mass. It is, in other words, enveloping but accommodating. Again, the air also does this, but the water helps us *feel* it. Poet Charles Tomlinson evokes the feeling of fluid parting and closing, in 'Swimming Chenango Lake'. The water, torn by his moving body, 'flows-to behind him,' healing as it does.

While mountains can certainly evoke the sublime, this intimate parting and joining is unique to fluid. It rightly gives the impression that we are not simply in the water, like a marble in a box – we are part of it; for a little while, we *are* it, and it moves as we move, just as we are pushed and pulled by currents.

This has led many to treat the water as a god or womb – something grand and exulted that one returns to. Novelist John Updike plays with this idea: in 'Lifeguard', one of his short story's characters is a young divinity student and lifeguard, who sees himself as a priest, overseeing the bathers worshipping in the waters. 'We enter the sea with a shock; our skin and blood shout in protest. But in that instant that leap, past, what do we find? Ecstasy and buoyancy.' The sea is a savage, wrathful god, which will absorb us (whether we like it or not).

In 'The Swimmer', Mary Oliver swaps Updike's New Testament ocean for a more pagan, maternal sea, in which 'every wall was water'.

Naturalist Ann Zwinger, in *A Desert Country Near the Sea*, describes this life under 'the silken tent' of the waves: 'how simple it is for those who pivot or rasp, supported and fed, adrift in an infinite womb . . . suspended easily in this friendly bath without having to battle the incessant pull of gravity.' Whether or not we, as adults, can actually recall being in utero is still being debated by psychologists and neuroscientists. But the feeling of water certainly suggests the metaphor: a fluid space we are vitally part of, which literally takes the weight off our feet. 'Reaching the water again, one smiles,' writers Tom Farber in *On Water*. 'To come back down to the ocean is to reexperience an essential memory trace, something one has known well, to recall that one has been trying to remember.'

Like Schopenhauer, the French author Romain Rolland was a devotee of Indian spirituality. Writing to Sigmund Freud, Rolland used a telling phrase to describe this oneness of ancient religions: 'oceanic'.

Question: Think of well-known rituals, fairy tales, blockbuster films. What is the role of water in each? How do they use water's size, power, chaos, darkness, depth?

Falling Into the World

What is the sublime telling us? For all this metaphysical talk, the sublime is not a secret universe, invisible to the ordinary eye. Instead, the sublime is a revelation of ordinary human contradiction:

the reality of our solitude and smallness, together with the intimation of safety and immensity. We are isolated and feeble, yet somehow joined with a world of security and strength.

Taken off the land and dumped into a few feet of water, Homo sapiens is a clumsy species. Even if we are confident swimmers, the water's enveloping power and caprice are intimidating. Particularly in the ocean – but pools too can challenge gifted swimmers – we confront the borders of our territory. We are, as philosopher Mark Rowlands puts it in *Running With the Pack*, 'big-arsed apes'. Great at running, not so good at swimming.

This is a recognition of what philosophers call 'finitude': the basic fact of limitation. To exist at all is to be a definite *this*, and not something else. However free we are, we cannot escape basic biology – *these* limbs, lungs and blood, *this* universe of force and gravity. More importantly, we cannot escape our mortality: pain and death will come to all of us, and no one can die on our behalf. Finitude is the recognition that we are fundamentally limited in time and space: small, easily broken things, whose clocks are always ticking.

This is why the sublime includes emotions like fear, shock, awe – they warn us that our puny bodies are in danger.

And yet the sublime also includes joy. Why? Partly because we are safe. Even if we are frightened, this is not abject terror – it becomes a buzz, instead of a warning horror. Meanwhile, gravity is put on hold. We are literally buoyed, and physically united with worldly stuff. We are part of the cosmos and its necessities. This need not suggest the divinity or womblike return noted by philosophers, novelists and poets – Rolland's 'oceanic feeling'. Instead, it is the recognition that, for all our weakness and isolation, we are strong, secure, and part of something bigger than our feeble selves.

The sublime slow lane.

Sigmund Freud, in *Civilization and its Discontents*, tried to capture Rolland's 'oceanic feeling' with a line from *Hannibal*, by the German dramatist Christian Dietrich Grabbe: 'we cannot fall out of the world.' This is the philosophical message of the sublime: for all our frailty, we are in this world, right now. It might be dangerous or baffling, but the world can be savoured. We can *feel* its immensity and potency.

In other words, the sublime is an introduction to the halfway house of human existence. It highlights our unique relation to the world: distant enough to see it from afar as something 'other', close enough to be moved and shaken. By threatening us, it stimulates. And, by keeping us secure, it allows us to enjoy this stimulation. Exercise, in this, is a chance to savour the precariousness of life – before we fall out of the world for good.

9. Oneness

Yoga: once an exotic rite for mystics, now a suburban hobby in church halls and gymnasiums. Stretches, belly breaths and chants. Ancient (and awkward) poses with odd animal names, enjoyed by Lycra-clad mothers and post-*matcha* tea hipsters alike.

For all their strangeness, meditative exercises like yoga, t'ai chi and sometimes Pilates can offer a distinctive calm. They encourage familiarity with one's own body, and then transcend this with an impression of 'oneness' with the world. They are more than sports to tone bums: they afford a brief liberation from the burden of being an 'I'.

A Happy Corpse

A suburban church hall, early evening. The cream-carpeted room is quiet – not even a clock ticking. (The *Hatha* yoga instructor has removed it.)

There are twelve of us: from a tanned twenty-something in short shorts, earlier chatting to her friend about who 'got with' whom, to a sixty-something veteran yoga couple, who have studied with this instructor for fifteen years.

My seven-year-old son was with me, but opted out of yoga in favour of comics and three trips to the toilet in the foyer. (Something to do with a chicken-and-pineapple pizza, and lemon meringue pie, stuffed in after school.)

I am doing the Cat pose: on all fours, my back curved upwards, head down. At the instructor's command, I look up, inhale and push my right leg out and up behind me; then exhale, look down, and pull my right knee in towards my chest. This is the *Vyaghrasana*, or Tiger pose. Soon we turn to the Cobra and Locust poses.

For all the talk of familiar animals, yoga seems a strange beast. *Yogis* and *yoginis* – male and female practitioners, respectively – might see the classes as normal, but this is chiefly familiarity. The long, full yoga breaths – beginning in the stomach, then in the chest – are unusual. The chants, like 'Om', are primal in sound, but mean little to most Westerners. The poses are often awkward, sometimes comical. In the Cobra, I look like I am trapped beneath an invisible (Indian) elephant, trying to leverage myself to safety using only my free limbs and a look of smug calm.

Yoga, in short, looks weird.

And yet it actually *feels* normal to me. Take the basic Warrior II pose of *Ashtanga Vinyasa* yoga, or Dynamic yoga, which I practise on another day in a first-floor boxing gym, amongst stacks of gloves and posters of Muhammed Ali. The Warrior pose is a lunge: right foot forward, leg bent at the knee; left leg straight back. Each arm is straight out, in opposite directions. As I struggle to hold my hands out straight without shaking; as my hips strain while I lengthen my lunge; as I work against gravity to keep my torso upright – in short, as I contort myself unnaturally – it feels pleasantly natural. This is not simply because the lunge is like an old karate stance. As I hold myself in the Warrior, I feel like I am *supposed* to pose this way. Not arms adjacent to one another; not both legs straight; not hips forward – *exactly* as I am, right now. For all my effort, I am at ease.

This calm returns later in the class. After the animals: zombies. *Shavasana*, or Corpse pose. Flat on my back, eyes closed, feet apart, hands away from the waist, palms upwards. At the teacher's instruction, I imagine my left hand, elbow, shoulder, relaxing one by one. Then the whole arm. I do the same for my left leg, and the left side of my torso and face. Then the right side. Then my whole body. Meanwhile, I am taking big belly breaths.

Confession: While in Corpse pose, my mind wandered. I imagined my whole body, then a chalk outline around it.

Again, there is nothing normal about *Shavasana*. Lying on my back is ordinary, but not in a room full of incense, heavy-breathing strangers, and at someone else's prompt. Yet the feeling afterwards is quite natural, as if I have claimed (or reclaimed) something that always belonged to me.

Likewise in t'ai chi, in which I punch, kick and throw at geological speeds: it becomes a slow, martial meditation, instead of a brutal attack or defence. Indeed, I have felt this relaxation in karate itself, as we stretch and breathe before class: a surreal combination of sore joints and calmness, which tranquillizes one before and after the scraps.

This is a physical pleasure, but also a mental one: like coming home after a long holiday, and looking at one's house anew – only the house is *me*.

What is going on?

The Mini-theatre of Me

The most obvious pleasure is muscular. If yoga's Warrior pose or t'ai chi's Cat stance look strange, it is partly because they are designed to use muscle groups we often ignore. For many, a typical day includes sitting – driving, typing, travelling on a train, watching television, browsing the internet – and a little movement, depending on our vocation: walking up foyer steps, picking up children, sawing and hammering wood, drawing, and so on. Then there are the most common exercises: walking, jogging, swimming, tennis, football. Even when we are physically adventurous, it is rare to really *feel* the individual muscles and their relationships. The way we stand, walk, sit – each requires countless motor skills, subtle and gross. But we are not aware of them: they are reflexes and habits.

As a result, our daily routines are often mute testimonies of our psyche and society. Gait, stance, accent, gestures, they are all what the French sociologist Pierre Bourdieu called the *habitus*. The *habitus* demonstrates not only our individual quirks, but also upbringing, schooling and professional life. The body, in other words, is a kind of fleshy record: an inscription of our private anxieties (and joys) and public achievements (and failures).

Question: Which muscles are tense right now? Which are relaxed? Ask yourself this question a few times a day, and see how your body parts are underused and overused.

Slow stretching often works to bring back awareness of the body; by making conscious what is usually unconscious. Not just visually, but kinaesthetically, from within. This is important in all new exercises and sports, as we move from novice clumsiness to competence. But yoga, in particular, offers a very precise, patient inventory of the flesh, and what it carries – what yoga scholar Richard Freeman, in *The Mirror of Yoga*, describes as a 'minitheater' for the body and psyche. In the Warrior pose, for example, various muscles are suddenly noticeable: in the hips and inner thighs as I lunge, in my shoulder blades as my arm stretches out, in my shoulder as I pivot my arm left or right. I can feel the weakness in my shoulders, from years of hunching over textbooks and notebooks, the ache in my neck, from sleeping badly in a week of hot summer nights and kids with a stomach bug. (It was not the pizza and lemon meringue after all.)

The *Vinyasa* sequences, like the forms of t'ai chi and other martial arts, heighten these feelings by working complementary muscle groups: in the Cat and Tiger, alongside pressure on my hands and wrists, I feel the tension in the front of my throat, lower back, and lower stomach; then in the back of my neck and shoulders, the broad length of my back. 'Every turn, every spiral, every extension, has to be tempered by a counterturn, a counterspiral,' Freeman continues. 'Every instruction or technique, at the right time, will need a counterinstruction or technique to find openness and balance.' This is also true of t'ai chi, with its Taoist theories of *yin* and *yang*, forces and counterforces. By literally seeking balance, I am also becoming more familiar with my body's intricate parts, and how they bear witness to my life. It is a reacquaintance with the habits of the *habitus*.

Meditation, whether in *Shavasana* or another relaxed pose, can consolidate this new familiarity. Building on the kinaesthetic awareness developed during the exercises, I concentrate on one body part at a time, then slowly put the parts together in my mind. Combined with the stretches, this reflection leaves me with a vivid picture of my own body – a picture that is not only seen, but felt.

This is partly why I left the hall more at ease. Not because the exercises of yoga were somehow 'normal', but because their abnormality nudged me to become more intimate with my own body. Bodybuilders, as we have seen, develop new visual patterns; give themselves the aesthetic experience of revised bodily form. Likewise for anyone who builds muscle and loses fat. But the pleasure is often literally superficial; as if from the outside. Gentle exercise, like stretching and breathing, does this from the inside. In yoga's strange poses, and meditation, I was able to remember all the muscular quirks I normally forget. I was more aware of the incidents and accidents that define me. In other words, I felt like I was more *myself*.

This is 'more' in two senses. First, in that I have a heightened sensation of my bodily practices, and the lifestyle they reflect – the *habitus* of Bourdieu.

But second, in exercise I can experience a richer conception of myself. It is an imagined *internal* world, which parallels the conventional world of sweat, skin and countless other surfaces. It is a portrait – admittedly a skewed and sketchy one – of the normally hidden architecture of muscles, sinews, blood flows and breath.

In yoga, this is turned into a metaphysical vision. There is the flesh, which we can see and feel normally, then there is the 'subtle body', which is conceived as a secondary world of more ethereal 'organs'. And it can seem immense. The body is treated as a microcosm of universal forces: its development echoes the physical and metaphysical levels of the cosmos. For example, in the eyes, says the *Advaya-Taraka-Upanishad*, 'there is a replica of the sun and the moon'. Likewise in t'ai chi, with its talk of *chi*, the Taoist notion of life force. The same principles that flow throughout the universe are also at work in the body. And knowledge of one's guts and limbs provides an intimacy with the laws of politics, ethics and statecraft. 'He who values his body more than dominion over the empire,' wrote Lao Tzu in the *Tao Te Ching*, 'can be entrusted with the empire.'

The point is not that these traditional philosophies and exercises are accurate descriptions of the cosmos – that there really are forces like *prana* or *chi*, and the 'organs' or 'meridians' they pool within. The point is that this increased sensitivity to one's body is also a mental exercise: a labour of imagination. By stretching meticulously and patiently, and meditating on the body's tensions, we can engage in a creative act. As we contort ourselves, and then meditate upon our flesh, we conceive a more elaborate idea of usually forgotten organs and tissue. This should not, and need not, replace proper physiological knowledge. Instead, it is a kind of interior decoration, only the 'home' is our own viscera. It is ours, not simply through accident, but through physical and mental labour. We are *making* ourselves at home in our insides.

I Am Ghee

But there is more to the pleasure of meditation than this existential clarity and inner vividness. Often, what accompanies exercise is the bliss, not of finding oneself bodily, but precisely the opposite: losing oneself – a kind of blissful abandon.

As it happens, bliss is actually at the heart of yoga. This is not the ecstasy of late-night clubbing or luxury tea. The Sanskrit word, *samadhi*, means wholeness or unity. It is a state of tranquil oneness, common to many mystical states.

The Indian sage Patanjali gave Indian civilization the first treatise devoted to yoga's philosophy and practice. In his first- or second-century *Yoga-Sutra*, he describes yoga as 'the restriction of the fluctuations of consciousness'. In *Raja* yoga (also known as Classical or *Ashtanga* yoga), we move away from the interruptions and intrusions of ordinary life. This yoga has 'eight limbs', starting with moral and bodily discipline, then moving to posture and breathing, sense withdrawal, concentration, meditation and finally ecstasy. (The last stage has various grades, from a kind of pleasant awareness to full-fledged enlightenment.)

Samadhi arises, said Patanjali, because consciousness is moving away from physical nature, toward the ideal self. So the point of the Cat and the Corpse is a unity with myself, only this self has nothing to do with my chubby thighs in compression tights, or the beef salad I had for dinner. This self is transcendent: spiritual, absolute, eternal. In this state, argued Patanjali, I avoid habit and memory – which trap me in material cause and effect – and become a kind of timeless, changeless being, what the yoga master described as 'unchanging Awareness'.

Not all schools of yoga agree with Patanjali's ideas, which are straightforwardly dualistic: nature on one side, the transcendent self on the other. In fact, most schools of yoga kept his 'eight limbs', but committed to what is called in philosophy 'monism': the world is one. In many of the medieval yoga traditions, there was no great division between body and mind, self and world. If all is one, then *everything*

Serpentine flexibility: a statue of Patanjali.

in life – food, drink, sex, love – can be transformed to achieve some bliss and enlightenment.

In *Hatha* yoga, for example, the body is 'spiritualized': the circulation of life force (*prana*) releases serpent energy (*kundalini*), which transmutes brute flesh into something more divine. While breathing heavily on my rainbow stripe towel, I was actually making my body 'adamantine'. (Fans of the superhero Wolverine, take note.)

In *Bhakti* yoga, devotion to a god brings the *yogi* or *yogini* out of brute egotism. Adoration of the divine is actually a love of the cosmos itself. 'By unswerving devotion, he comes to Me,' says god Vishnu in the *Uddhava-Gita*, 'the great Lord of all the worlds, the Absolute, the ultimate cause, the origin and end of all.'

Tip: Check out the philosophy of your yoga school. You might find it is quite foreign to many of your beliefs, about the body, nature and the mind. Likewise for any alternative or traditional art.

As this suggests, yoga is an ancient tradition, and contains varieties of belief and ritual. But regardless of the school, all yoga involves the transcendence of the ordinary 'I'. Hence the phrase 'the wheel of yoga': all the spokes end in the same centre, ecstasy. In much of the Hindu tradition, this means overcoming the division between the subject and object; between everything 'in here' and everything 'out there'. At the highest levels, I no longer see myself as a thing amongst things. Instead, my 'self' and the world are unified. 'Just as ghee poured into ghee is still only ghee, or milk into milk,' says the *Goraksha-Paddhati*, or 'Tracks of Goraksha', 'so the *yogin* is but Reality.' This is *samadhi*.

I did not feel this joyful oneness in the church hall or local boxing gym – perhaps because Patanjali's 'fluctuations of consciousness' got the better of me. But I have felt it during karate (my school's grand-master was also a yoga student), and during t'ai chi. It is common amongst practitioners of meditation: not simply a calmness, but a feeling that one's 'I' has dissolved, dispersed. What is happening?

Goodbye to Things

Those who have enjoyed mystical states often describe them as 'beyond words'. Yoga masters often note that ecstasy is ineffable, inexplicable, indescribable – at best, it is hinted at by metaphors and symbols. The *Goraksha-Paddhati* speaks of *samadhi* as 'the vanishing of all ideation and the identity of all pairs-of-opposites'. In other words, this particular pleasure of yoga, and other kinds of medita-tion, resists words because language requires the very distinctions that ecstasy destroys.

But a clearer idea of the 'how' of ecstasy does not require a 'what'. We need not say exactly what *samadhi* is in order to describe how it comes about. Indeed, this is what yoga is for: the word comes from the same root as 'yoke', in English, and suggests joining, gathering together, reining in. In other words, yoga is a practical philosophy, designed to yoke the self to something bigger. Hindu scholar Georg Feuerstein, in his encyclopaedic *The Yoga Tradition*, describes this as 'the technology of ecstasy'.

Research suggests that the 'technology' of meditation works. One study, by Telles and Raghavendra, found definite changes in blood pressure, autonomic functions and brain blood flows during yoga. In particular, the scans suggest a clear difference between the earlier stages of focus, and later stages of what they call 'mental expansiveness' – a vivid, lucid consciousness, without the narrowness of normal concentration. Interestingly, yoga meditators often moved spontaneously from the former to the latter – echoing the movement of Patanjali's 'limbs'. In short: yoga is not just a 'state of mind', as if this were ethereal – it involves the whole physical and mental self.

Other research suggests the neurophysiological reasons for these changes of consciousness. In one study, neuroscientist Andrew Newberg and colleagues reported that meditators had busy frontal lobes – suggesting high concentration – but lazier parietal lobes. Like the prefrontal cortex, the parietal lobe is a coordinator. But it brings together sensory information, rather than dealing with planning and concepts. It is responsible for what Newberg and d'Aquili, in *The Mystical Mind*, call 'the self-world distinction'. For example, I can see my rainbow-stripe towel under me, feel its synthetic fuzz, and hear its muffled scraping against the carpet – the parietal lobe is what helps me to identify all this data as *one* thing, next to my hands. Victims of damage to the parietal lobe often have trouble identifying objects in space – they might see my towel, for example, but not know where it is. They are not *in* the world as we are.

This 'spacelessness' is exactly what meditation can cause – and pleasantly so. The decreased blood flow to the parietal lobes coincides with a very common part of *samadhi*: the impression that one has transcended the division of subject and object. So the meditator has no sense of things in the room; of being one object amongst others: towels, clocks, speakers playing New Age sounds of waves and rain. She has, quite literally, lost her perception of space, and everything in it. Newberg and d'Aquili describe this as 'the obliteration of the distinction between self and other.' It is a goodbye to things – including ourselves.

So meditation can offer a deeper, wider consciousness – a feeling that we have left the ego behind, and achieved a more transcendent state. Of course, this says nothing about what the universe actually *is* – monist or dualist, one or many, divine or otherwise. It is not a handshake with God. Instead, it is a brief emancipation from the experience of ourselves.

No Strings Attached

This oneness is partly why so many busy, stressed Westerners have taken up yoga and other meditations. These practices can relieve many of the anxieties that come with daily life: the 'attachments' spoken of by Hindu and Buddhist scholars. Both philosophies believe that everyday anguish is caused not by the world, but by our cravings for it – for our rigid categories, fixed ideals and narrow goals. We are needy or greedy subjects, in a world of objects. The point of yoga, in particular, is not necessarily a life of austere renunciation – although many Hindus take up this lifestyle – but one of psychological remoteness: giving up on being subjects (who crave) amongst objects (of craving). 'Do thy work in the peace of yoga and, free from selfish desires, be not moved in success or in failure,' said Krishna in the *Bhagavad Gita*, one of the most popular Hindu texts, and an early yoga primer. 'Yoga is evenness of mind'.

Alongside meditation's more obvious muscular and circulatory training, this non-attachment might provide various health benefits, like lower blood pressure and decreased stress. Several recent reviews of the research come to the same conclusion: there is no clear-cut evidence of yoga's medical virtues. Aside from aches and strains, it is certainly not harmful, but it cannot replace conventional medicine. Nonetheless, the research suggests that many *yogis* and *yoginis* clearly find in yoga a tranquillity lacking in their office cubicles and living rooms. And this can, for many, lead to fewer feelings of anxiety, as well as lower levels of the stress hormone, cortisol. The feeling of being 'unborn, unchanging, and unsullied by all objects', as the *Katha Upanishad* puts it, is a brief relief from our barbed ties to the world.

Yoga teacher and psychologist Anna Evans has also suggested that it can encourage us to be more comfortable with the ambiguity. We realize the shifty nature of perception and identity; the blurred outlines that often seem so clear.

This might seem like shallow consolation: after all, once the feelings of oneness subside, the subject and its objects return. We are again reminded of our own doubts and appetites, and the world's unreachable joys. But the point of bliss in meditation is not to do away with the world entirely and for good, but to put it in perspective. Having seen the dissolution of our concepts – 'out there' and 'in here', 'me' and 'you', 'what I want' and 'what I am' – we return to ordinary life with a slightly less panicky or harried frame of mind. We realize the contrived or contorted nature of our usual attachments. Meditation, in other words, is like an unpicker in sewing: it allows us to change the shape of our attitudes, by taking life apart at the seams.

Question: How often do you feel nagged, seduced or besieged by stuff? In what things – houses, cars, money, luxury goods, desks, kitchens – do your anxieties live?

Yoga Butt, But . . .

Do we need the 'metaphysical' parts of meditation to enjoy its bliss? The short answer is 'no'.

For example, one careful study by University of Western Sydney researcher Caroline Smith and colleagues reported that *Hatha* yoga and muscle-relaxation techniques had very similar health benefits. At the end of a ten-week programme, most participants in both exercises were calmer and less anxious. By sixteen weeks, the groups were basically the same, though the muscle-relaxation group were much higher in 'social functioning, mental health and vitality'.

The point is not that yoga is dangerous for sanity, but that belief in mystical 'oneness' is not necessarily what brings on ecstasy, or eases stress. As we have seen, stretching, breathing and concentrating can be enough. Smith's study, along with other research, demonstrates that slow, careful stretching and relaxation are themselves kinds of meditation. What *Hatha yogis* and *yoginis* practise is a refined and tested version of this, combined with Hindu mythology, religion and philosophy. Likewise for Taoist ideas in t'ai chi, or any other esoteric philosophy of exercise. In short: we need not believe in serpent energy or *chi* to feel freer.

However, we *do* need to pause, breathe and patiently focus, and to do this regularly. In other words, meditation is at the heart of yoga, and other slow or still exercises like t'ai chi, or stretching and breathing before vigorous exercise. Taking up yoga purely for muscles will certainly lead to improved flexibility and strength. As model and famous *yogini* Christy Turlington told *Time*, 'I have friends who simply want to have a yoga butt.' And there is nothing wrong with a pert bum. But this is only the muscular dimension of the exercise. Without the right mindset, the psychological dimensions – from inner daydreaming, to oneness, to lowered anxiety – will be missed. We will have stretched bodies, but not stretched minds.

Tip: *Ecstasy requires, not religious devotion, but calm, patient commitment to concentration. Wanting a quick fix for stress is a problem not a solution.*

Nice body, but no bliss: mannequins advertising yoga sportswear.

Conclusion

Chad might not have read this far into the book. Not because he did badly at school, or scorns popular non-fiction, but because he does not value intellectual adventure and ethical growth. More specifically, he does not value *himself* for these things. In other words, Chad's failure is not because he lacks raw cognitive power, but because his existential ambitions are too low. He does not aspire to a fuller ideal of human wholeness. All his daily toil in the gym is not coupled with reflection, meditation or virtue.

To do better than the Chads of this world – or those anti-Chads, like Epigenes – we need not develop thirty-inch biceps or the ultra-marathon runner's hibernating-bear pulse. The ambition is not one of scale but of scope: enrolling *more* of our humanity into fitness. This might be, as with reverie, combining walking with the undistracted solitude to best enjoy it. It might be, as with flow, recognizing our faults to better commune with a tactile world. In each case, the point is to unite physical striving with the moods and mindsets that best give rise to effort, and arise from it. This is intelligent exercise, and it is as fun as it is fulfilling.

While some exercises are exotic, and some athletes elite, intelligent exercise is often best enjoyed as an ordinary, amateur pursuit. Yes, mountaineers like Joe Simpson and runners like Murakami are rare, even amongst climbers and joggers. But Darwin, for all his world-class scholarship, was not a world-class walker; *yogini* Christy Turlington is not known for her meticulous Hindu metaphysics. Common to the radical naturalist and the ex-model is not excellence in every field, but that very Greek desire: to be more than just a cogitating mind *or* posing body – to be whole.

For most of us, this balance has little to do with the Olympian's frenetic regimes, or even Chad's earnest gym ministrations. Instead, it is achieved by painstakingly putting together work, chores or study with physical training, and the leisure to reflect on each. In this, fitness is not an 'extra', but something braided into the sometimes-fraying strings of ordinary life. While we might be inspired by the Tour de France or Usain Bolt, intelligent exercise is more about riding to work in drizzling rush hour, having a quick shower, and letting the pumping blood invigorate our cubicled brain; more about the few miles of treadmill or track pounded after the kids are asleep and lunches made. To exercise intelligently is to develop an unusual fullness of character within the usual circumstances.

It is a truism that 'you get out what you put in'. This is certainly true of exercise. But with an exception: what we put in and take away are not always the same *kind* of thing. When we are committed to a more balanced life – a life without dualism – we can enjoy a kind of human alchemy: we put in raw muscular strain and agility, and get back some psychological gold. And vice versa: the price of a stronger arm or heart is a mind that can attend to racquet and ball, rock or road, with greater accuracy. Either way, intelligent exercise is always a to-and-fro. We are not defined by our mind or our body, but by their intimate congress.

While fitness is rightly challenging, this congress need not be a dreary duty, taken up to meet strangers' aesthetic standards, or simply to stave off illness. Yes, beauty and health are certainly important. But they can become external 'necessities' rather than internal pleasures and virtues. And in this, they can very quickly become tedious and alienating – no longer 'our' exercise, in other words. The point is to see fitness as a personal adventure, however painful or wearying, rather than solely as a commandment.

This idea of adventure is also a helpful reminder to try new sports and exercises. Of course it is important, for the sake of consistency, to be a regular in the gym, on the footpath or mats. But it is equally important to welcome novelty, particularly when it might complement our character. The brash bodybuilder might like to try rock climbing for humility, and the humble t'ai chi adept might try sprints or weights for pride. A Sunday bike-rider, deadened by weekdays at the desk, might take up walking alone for reverie. An anxious jogger can try yoga's calming oneness. The idea is to see exercise as a remedy for existential incompleteness, instead of just a way to postpone death or purchase sexiness with sweat.

For this reason, the message of this book is not 'just do it', with its ideal of thoughtless action. (Perfect for advertisers.) There is more than enough 'doing' going on, particularly in gyms. 'Just be' is little better, reflecting a kind of bovine quietude. My mantra of intelligent exercise is one that suggests movement, change, transformation: just *become* it. The 'it' is entirely up to each of us.

Homework

Part of the fun of writing this book has been exercising, then reflecting on exercise. Seeing how my slow footpath toddling, for example, seems in light of Murakami's marathons; scaling an urban wall, then reflecting on Harrer's ludicrous and numinous Eiger climb.

Here are a few of the books, essays and films that informed or inspired me, or kicked me in the pants to get fitter.

Introduction

The Coen Brothers' *Burn After Reading* (2008) is a wry, well-paced and very intelligent film – somewhere between satire and thriller. Its quiet mockery of the fitness industry is spot-on.

Alongside Plato's dialogues like *Phaedo* and *Phaedrus* (*Plato: The Collected Dialogues*, Princeton, 2005), René Descartes's *Meditations on First Philosophy* (*A Discourse on Method, Meditations and Principles*, Everyman, 1999) is *the* work of Western dualism. While not as elegant or eloquent as the Athenian's works, it's also quite readable in English.

If Plato and Descartes are the philosopher-kings of dualism, Merleau-Ponty is the emperor of embodiment. His masterwork is *Phenomenology of Perception* (Routledge and Kegan Paul, 1970) but

The World of Perception (Routledge, 2008) is an excellent short introduction to some of his ideas.

Martin Heidegger's *Being and Time* (Basil Blackwell, 1985) is one
of the most important philosophical books of the twentieth century.
It is also one of the most difficult. If you are interested in an intelligent and clear introduction, Hubert Dreyfus's *Being-in-the-World*
(MIT Press, 1991) is an excellent start.

Xenophon was not Greece's finest philosopher, but he is, today,
a perfect example of brains and brawn in the one curmudgeon. His
Conversations of Socrates (Penguin, 2004), for all its 'tut-tut' morality,
is a virtual 'second opinion' on Socrates and his city.

Reverie

For a short, well-informed and warm life of Darwin, try Tim M.
Berra's *Charles Darwin: The Concise Story of an Extraordinary
Man* (Johns Hopkins University Press, 2009). Janet Browne's
two-volume biography is generous in spirit and meticulous in detail
(Vintage, 2010).

Novelist and neuropsychologist Kylie Ladd has an excellent
essay on 'transient hypofrontality' (and creativity in general) in
the *Griffith Review*: www.griffithreview.com/edition-23-essentially-
creative/the-unexpected-idea

Pride

David Hume's *A Treatise of Human Nature* (Penguin, 2005) is arguably the most important work of philosophy in English. It is lucid, wise and often beautifully written.

Speaking of English, Robert Fagles's translations of Homer's *Iliad* (Penguin, 1991) and *Odyssey* (Penguin, 2006) are exemplary: gritty and graceful in equal measure.

Pindar's Victory Songs (John Hopkins University Press, 1980), written some two hundred years after Homer, are sometimes haunting portraits of athletic splendour. For every line of praise there is a word of caution: this, too, shall pass.

Sacrifice

J. R. R. Tolkien's essay 'On Fairy-Stories' (in *The Monster and the Critics*, HarperCollins, 2006) is a very thoughtful meditation on make-believe and fantasy from an author who knew a thing or two about imagination.

Sociologist Pierre Bourdieu is not an easy read. But his books, like *Pascalian Meditations* (Polity Press, 2000), are meticulous analyses of society; of its games, and their stakes. Richard Jenkins's *Pierre Bourdieu* (Routledge, 2002) is a helpful guide to these ideas.

Beauty

A succinct introduction to the classical ideal in Plato and Aristotle is *Greek Aesthetic Theory* by J. G. Warry (Routledge, 2012). John Boardman's well-illustrated *Greek Art* (Thames & Hudson, 1996) complements Warry nicely.

This BBC4 video, 'Phi's the limit', sings the praises of the golden ratio: www.geomarkowsky.com/wordpress/wp-content/uploads/2012/05/GoldenRatio.pdf. 'Misconceptions about the Golden Ratio', by George Markovsky, debunks many *phi* claims: www.umcs.maine.edu/~markov/GoldenRatio.pdf.

The world of bodybuilding flesh is exposed in the documentaries *Pumping Iron* I (1977) and II (1985), and Sam Fussell's memoir *Muscle* (Poseidon Press, 1991). A more literary and idiosyncratic story of beauty and its pathologies is Yukio Mishima's *Sun and Steel* (Kodansha, 2003).

John Dewey's *Art as Experience* (Minton, Balch and Company, 1934) is a classic modern work of aesthetics: readable, straightforward and in no way dated. Dewey is helpfully democratic about the enjoyment of beauty.

Humility

Mihaly Csikszentmihalyi's *Flow* (Rider, 2002) deftly highlights the joy of skilful striving. It makes sense of everything from climbing, to chess, to dance.

Joe Simpson's *Touching the Void* (Vintage, 1998) is a thriller of a story, and an existentialist classic. The 2003 documentary, directed by Kevin Macdonald, is also excellent. Heinrich Harrer's *The White Spider* (HarperCollins, 2010), which inspired Simpson, is still a gripping read. Both reveal the ordinary human moments in extraordinary feats.

Capturing the naive determination of youth, Nadia Comaneci's *Letters to a Young Gymnast* (Basic Books, 2009) is moving but also very illuminating.

Pain

This short McGill University video explains Ronald Melzack's discoveries of pain: www.youtube.com/watch?v=KRFanGInvlc.

Martial Arts and Philosophy: Beating and Nothingness (Open Court, 2010), which I edited with Graham Priest, has a number of popular essays on martial arts and philosophy (surprise, surprise). Kevin Krein's 'Sparring With Emptiness' is a good introduction to the existentialist idea of freedom.

While writing this chapter, I was informed by Steve Bein's 'Understanding Quality and Suffering Through the Martial Arts', which is part of a new collection Graham Priest and I are editing for Routledge.

Mischa Merz is a writer, artist and Golden Gloves winner. Her book *Bruising* (Vulgar Press, 2009) is an illuminating portrayal of the martial arts (for men and women).

On pain and its meanings in ballet, see Darren Aronofsky's haunting film *Black Swan* (2010), starring Natalie Portman.

Consistency

Alasdair MacIntyre's *After Virtue* (Duckworth, 1997) remains a standard reference for modern ideas of virtue, and the value of narratives. A timely, wide-ranging and simply written (but not simplistic) book.

What I Talk About When I Talk About Running, by Haruki Murakami (Vintage, 2009), is a quirky look into the runner's mind, as well as a great story of real-world virtue. Mark Rowlands's *Running With the Pack* (Granta, 2013) is less extreme in its jogging but far more profound in its ideas.

For 'get out there and DO IT (for hours)' reading, try *The Extra Mile* (Rodale, 2006) by Pam Reed or *Ultramarathon Man* by Dean Karnazes (Jeremy P. Tarcher, 2006).

The Sublime

A Philosophical Enquiry into the Origin of Our Ideas of the Sublime and the Beautiful, by Edmund Burke, is a refreshingly modern work: sensitive to awe, but wary of the supernatural.

Arthur Schopenhauer's *The World as Will and Idea* is less realistic, but gives a fuller impression of the immersion – literal and metaphorical – we feel in water.

Laurel Blossom's *Splash!* is, as far as I know, the only collection of swimming writing. Poetry, essays, short fiction, novel extracts: a fantastic anthology, which really nudged me back to the locals pools.

While James Bradley's *The Penguin Book of the Ocean* is not all about swimming, it is an expertly-chosen selection of sea writings, from Coleridge's *Rime of the Ancient Mariner* to Tim Winton on surfing.

Thomas Farber's *On Water* is an extraordinary meditation on this needful liquid stuff.

I recommend Don Cheever's short story 'The Swimmer' (available in Blossom's anthology) for its portrait of water and flight from reality. The 1968 film, starring Burt Lancaster in his swimming trunks, is excellent.

Oneness

Newberg and d'Aquili's work on the neuroscience of meditation is collected in *The Mystical Mind* (Augsburg Fortress, 1999). Andrew Newberg discusses meditation here: www.youtube.com/watch?v=67YjAxagE7A.

The standard Western reference for yoga in English is Georg Feuerstein's *The Yoga Tradition* (Hohm Press, 2001). Holding up this oversized, encyclopaedic textbook is a workout in itself.

The *Upanishads* (Penguin, 2004) include some of the earliest Hindu writings on yoga, but can also be read for curiosity and pleasure. Likewise for the *Bhagavad Gita* (Oxford University Press, 2008). (Selections from both are included in *The Yoga Tradition*, but stand-alone paperbacks are readily available.)

Acknowledgements

Several friends, colleagues and strangers were generous with their ideas and words. Thanks to: James Bradley, Anna Evans, Tom Farber, Clint Greagen, Kylie Ladd, David Lebedoff, Mike Menzies, Mischa Merz, Heather Moritz, David Morley, Greg Roberts, Mark Rowlands, Joe Simpson. Thanks also to The School of Life and my Pan Macmillan editors.

Picture Acknowledgements

The author and publisher would like to thank the following for permission to reproduce the images used in this book:

Page viii Brad Pitt in *Burn After Reading*, 2008 © REX / Snap Stills

Page 7 John McEnroe at Wimbledon, 1980 © Steve Powell / Getty Images

Page 13 C. W. Eckersberg, *Socrates and Alcibiades*, 1813–1816 © Thorvaldsens Museum. Photographer Hans Petersen

Pages 20–21 The Sandwalk © Ted Grant / Wikimedia Commons

Page 28 Darwin riding his horse, Tommy © The Darwin Collection, Cambridge University Library, MS.DAR.225:116

Page 31 Spider web © Helen Gladman

Page 43 Portrait engraving of David Hume © Universal History Archive / Getty Images

Page 48 Hoplitodromos © Marie-Lan Nguyen / Wikimedia Commons

Pages 58–59 Drouin schoolboys playing cricket, Drouin, Victoria c.1944 © Jim Fitzpatrick / National Library of Australia, an24280176

Page 63 The Doubles final in Lahore, Pakistan © Photo courtesy of the National Archive UK, CO 1069-515-3

Page 73 The *Doryphoros* of Polyclitus. Cast in Pushkin Museum, Moscow © Shakko / Wikimedia Commons

Pages 90–91 The Eiger © NHPA / Photoshot

Page 109 Karen Kain and Denys Ganio in *Carmen*, 1975 © Lipnitzki / Roger Viollet / Getty Images

Page 115 Boston Marathon, 1980 © David Madison / Getty Images

Page 121 Murakami stretching © Patrick Fraser / Guardian News & Media Ltd 2008

Page 151 Patanjali © Jayne Jonas

All other images provided courtesy of the author.

Notes

Notes

Notes

Notes

Notes

TOOLS FOR THINKING

A NEW RANGE OF NOTEBOOKS, PENCILS, CARDS
& GIFTS FROM THE SCHOOL OF LIFE

Good thinking requires good tools. To complement our classes,
books and therapies, THE SCHOOL OF LIFE now offers a range of
stationery products and gifts that are both highly useful and
stimulating for the eye and mind.

THESCHOOLOFLIFE.COM

TWITTER.COM/THESCHOOLOFLIFE

If you enjoyed this book, we'd encourage you to check out other titles in the series:

Also available:

Other series from THE SCHOOL OF LIFE:

LIFE LESSONS FROM GREAT THINKERS:
BERGSON, BYRON, FREUD, HOBBES, KIERKEGAARD, NIETZSCHE

If you'd like to explore more good ideas for everyday life, THE SCHOOL OF LIFE runs a regular programme of classes, weekends, secular sermons and events in London and other cities around the world.

Browse our shop and visit:

THESCHOOLOFLIFE.COM
TWITTER.COM/THESCHOOLOFLIFE

panmacmillan.com
twitter.com/panmacmillan